How to
PC up and running

OTHER TITLES BY THE SAME AUTHOR

How to get your PC up and running

by

Ian Sinclair

BERNARD BABANI (publishing) LTD

THE GRAMPIANS

SHEPHERDS BUSH ROAD

LONDON W6 7NF

ENGLAND

PLEASE NOTE

Although every care has been taken with the production of this book to ensure that any projects, designs, modifications and/or programs, etc., contained herewith, operate in a correct and safe manner and also that any components specified are normally available in Great Britain, the Publishers and Author(s) do not accept responsibility in any way for the failure (including fault in design) of any project, design, modification or program to work correctly or to cause damage to any equipment that it may be connected to or used in conjunction with, or in respect of any other damage or injury that may be so caused, nor do the Publishers accept responsibility in any way for the failure to obtain specified components.

Notice is also given that if equipment that is still under warranty is modified in any way or used or connected with home-built equipment then that warranty may be void.

British Library Cataloguing in Publication Data:

A catalogue record for this book is available from the British Library

ISBN 0 85934 446 0

Cover Design by Gregor Arthur
Cover Illustration by Adam Willis
Printed and Bound in Great Britain by Cox & Wyman Ltd., Reading

ABOUT THIS BOOK

Choosing and using a computer, particularly your first PC, can be difficult, mainly because there is so much to think about. A PC is not a simple device like a washing machine or a video recorder, and when the delivery firm leaves these large boxes at your door you are on your own. You are even more on your own earlier in the process when you make the decision to buy or not, and which model to go for.

This book is intended to ease your path to getting that PC up and running, starting at the obvious question — why do you want to buy a PC? There is a wealth of advice that you don't find elsewhere, like how to choose a good site for your computer and how to organise your unpacking. Connecting up is dealt with in detail, with illustrations of plugs and sockets that you have to be able to recognise. You will learn how to find what programs have been placed in your computer by the suppliers and how to add others. Finally, you will find an account of the types of software programs that you can add to make the PC useful to **you**.

A few computer suppliers provide good clear manuals, but only too often all that you get is a vast set of manuals designed for computer buffs, with no clue as to what is really important for you. Worse still, you may get a few photocopied pages that appear to be badly translated from Japanese.

Use this book as a guide to your first steps in computing and you are less likely to fall flat on your face. You will know why you are buying the machine and where you intend to site it. You will know how to connect the parts together and how to make the machine come to life with its software. You will also learn some of the language of computing so that you can make sense of the advertisements in the magazines, and how to tell if you are getting good value for money.

If your first computer is likely to be a low-cost second-hand or 'surplus' bargain, you are not neglected, because this book tells you what constitutes a bargain in computer terms, and exposes some of the 'bargains' that would be expensive at any price.

Whether you are eight or eighty, going for your first-ever computer or replacing a very old model, this book has advice and useful hints for you.

Ian Sinclair

Autumn 1997

ABOUT THE AUTHOR

Ian Sinclair was born in 1932 in Tayport, Fife, and graduated from the University of St. Andrews in 1956. In that year, he joined the English Electric Valve Co. in Chelmsford, Essex, to work on the design of specialised cathode-ray tubes, and later on small transmitting valves and TV transmitting tubes.

In 1966, he became an assistant lecturer at Hornchurch Technical College, and in 1967 joined the staff of Braintree College of F.E. as a lecturer. His first book, "Understanding Electronic Components" was published in 1972, and he has been writing ever since, particularly for the novice in Electronics or Computing. The interest in computing arose after seeing a Tandy TRS80 in San Francisco in 1977, and of his 180 published books, about half have been on computing topics, starting with a guide to Microsoft Basic on the TRS80 in 1979.

He left teaching in 1984 to concentrate entirely on writing, and has also gained experience in computer typesetting, particularly for mathematical texts. He has recently visited Seattle to see Microsoft at work, and to remind them that he has been using Microsoft products longer than most Microsoft employees can remember.

ACKNOWLEDGEMENTS

I would like to thank the friendly and helpful staff of Text 100 Ltd. for providing the MS-DOS and Windows 95 software on which this book has been based, and Word 97 on which it was composed and typeset.

TRADEMARKS

Microsoft, MS-DOS, Windows, Windows 95 and NT are either registered trademarks or trademarks of Microsoft Corporation.

All other brand and product names used in this book are recognised as trademarks, or registered trademarks, of their respective companies.

Contents

Preface

Are you just about to unpack your first computer? Perhaps you are just awaiting delivery, or you have not yet decided what to do about buying your first computer. Whatever stage you have arrived at, this book aims to help you in choosing, buying, unpacking and setting up your first PC. This book is unashamedly aimed at the novice, and though some users with a little experience might find a few tips useful, it's not intended for the PC user with several years of experience.

In particular, I want to help the would-be user who is convinced that the computer requires degree-level knowledge and years of experience, or who feels that his/her age is against him/her. Certainly if you are under 7 you might not be so handy with a keyboard, and there are few PC beginners over the age of 95, but that leaves plenty of you in-between these extremes.

There are experts who will tell you that none of this is needed, and that computers are so simple now that anyone can set them up and start using them. That's not true. A computer is not like an electric kettle or even like a TV receiver — and let's remember that not all owners of video-cassette recorders know how to program them to record Monday's Coronation Street every week. A computer is by far the most complicated piece of electronics ever to be offered in shops, and to pretend otherwise is foolish. You will be offered some help if you buy a new TV, and you certainly need some if you buy a computer. You need help even more if you buy an older model of computer.

You could, of course, get tuition at £15 per hour or so, but do you need it? Your first steps with a computer are not like taking driving lessons, because you are not a menace to anyone if you are a novice in charge of a computer. The main thing to understand is that short of pouring your tea all over it or hitting it with a hammer, there is not much that can

damage it that would not just as surely kill off your TV or
video machine. This book costs less than one short hour of
instruction. There's no contest really, is there?

In addition, what you learn at your own pace and making
your own mistakes, is what you remember. This book is a
guide — it helps you to do what is correct, but it doesn't
stop you from experimenting and finding out for yourself
using your own machine.

1 Why do you want a PC?

If you were thinking of buying a car, you would have had some thoughts on why you needed a car. Some things would be obvious, such as the facts that the buses stop running after 6.00 p.m. and the nearest railway station is twelve miles away. Having decided to buy, other items might need a little more thought. Do you want to tow a caravan? Do you want to keep running costs low? Do you just want to impress the neighbours?

You certainly need to think just as hard about why you want to buy a computer and what you want from a computer. Unlike a car, a computer can be put to a huge variety of uses. Unlike a car, the computer is totally useless by itself — it needs sets of coded instructions called *applications* (or *programs*) to make it useful. The heavy bits that are connected together are called the *hardware* and the applications (which nowadays come stored on compact discs) are called *software*. You need to think about both.

There is one totally wrong reason for buying a computer, and that's because everyone else you know has one. That's no reason for buying anything, and particularly a computer, because unless you have a reason to justify it, you are not likely to want to use it or to learn how to make it useful to you. That's not to say that wanting to learn about using a computer is not a valid reason for owning one, because once you have had some experience you will probably have a much better idea of what you want to use it for. It's seldom too early, and never too late, to start, and once you have a few computing miles on your clock you will find it easier to keep up with the startling rate of progress. There's nothing wrong about buying a computer just for curiosity, either.

Wanting to learn is the first reason, then, for many people, particularly when they have seen others using computers successfully. Don't be put off by stories about losing work

3

Why do you want a PC?

or the network always being down — these are office horror stories, and you will be in charge of your own computer, not dependent on one that everyone else is using or connected to. You can learn much faster on your own, learning from your mistakes, than in a class where you will always be kept on the right track, copying what someone else is doing.

Word processing

More computers are used for word processing than for anything else, and it's rare nowadays to see a typewriter being used in an office. Word processing is to typing as a combine harvester is to a scythe and pitchfork, and the change that it has made to all sorts of *documents* (computerspeak for anything on paper that started on a computer) is immense. If you want an example, compare a parish magazine of today with one of twenty years ago. Gone are the days of poorly typed pages full of alterations, dotted with correcting fluid, irregular line lengths, hand-drawn diagrams, and misspellings. Gone also are the faint or over-inked duplicated sheets, sometimes in purple ink that faded out after a year.

Word processing is done using software, a word-processor application. This starts running when you command it (and we'll see how that's done later). When this application is running your screen looks like a sheet of paper, perhaps with some reminders at top and bottom. You type, and the words appear on the screen, looking just as they will on the paper. You can set the size of paper that you will use either before you type or after, it doesn't matter. You can delete a letter, word or phrase in an instant and type something else. You can rearrange your text, reversing the order of sentences or paragraphs without needing to re-type anything. You don't need to print anything on paper until it's as perfect as you can get it.

When you have finished your document, you can check the spelling. Some word processor applications will check the spelling as you type, putting a wavy red line under a misspelled word. Some will check grammar, but this is not yet done well enough to rely on except for finding things like omitted capital letters, missing commas or full stops, etc.

When the document looks exactly as you want it, you can *save* it, meaning that it is recorded as a file inside the computer. This is done using a gadget called a *hard drive* or hard disc, and anyone selling a computer will tell you that the larger the capacity of this hard drive the better. That's true, but when you start with your first computer you are not likely to need a vast amount of capacity. You must give the document a name so that it can be located. The name is its *filename*, and each document needs a filename that is its own, so that you can be sure of finding it again.

The useful thing about all this is that you never need to type the document again. If you want to make another document that is similar, perhaps with some names changed or material omitted or added you can start by *loading* your first document. When you request this action you will see a list of filenames appear on the screen, so that you can choose your document.

When the document appears, you can make the alterations and then save it using another filename. The first document is still stored unchanged in the hard drive, and you can get at it again any time you want. Your second document is now also stored and equally available.

If you use a word processor for your letters, for example, you will never again have to type your own name and address on a letter. If you often send a letter to a relative, you do not need to type that name and address, and you do not need to repeat items like *Dear Sue*, or *Love to all* or *With my sincere best wishes* and so on. You can base each letter on the one that you typed before, deleting the main message, but keeping the bits that don't change.

That's the simplest aspect of word processing, but it can extend much further. You can create documents that look as good as any printed material you have ever seen — and you can save a fortune in printing items like invitations to parties, weddings, christenings and so on. You can create mini-posters, menus, catalogues, advertising leaflets, magazine pages, whatever you want, and you can add drawings and pictures to your pages. Once you have taken the first step the others seem so much easier.

Desktop publishing (DTP)

Desktop publishing means producing documents that look as if they were produced by a professional printer. To some extent, the role of DTP has been taken over by the larger (and more expensive) word processing programs, but there are still several DTP programs at reasonable prices that are ideal for small-scale work, such as advertising fliers, menus, order of service sheets, all the way up to parish magazines and even larger publications.

Desktop publishing was made possible by two developments — the desktop computer and the laser printer, and to do justice to your DTP documents you really need a good laser printer, though some modern inkjet types can come very close in terms of quality.

Useful as DTP can be for the more flashy type of printing, you can do just as well for long plain documents, such as a complete book manuscript, with a top-level word processing program such as Microsoft Word.

Spreadsheets

Unlike word processing software which does the task that the typewriter and the printing press once did, there was never anything quite like a spreadsheet before small computers arrived. In fact when the first spreadsheet, called Visicalc, was demonstrated in 1978 some who saw it thought it was a trick, but many others bought a computer just so that they could use it.

A spreadsheet allows you to work with numbers, making tables. You could, if you wanted, create the familiar multiplication tables, but the spreadsheet, like all computer applications, allows you to decide for yourself what you want to do. You might, for example, enter a list of items and their cost price. As you do this, other columns in the sheet show the marked-up price, the VAT to be added and the final price. These extra columns are created by the spreadsheet application, and you do not have to type them. You simply enter the actions (like mark up by 50% and add 17.5% VAT) and leave all the rest to the spreadsheet to fill in.

If you need to work with rows and columns of words or numbers, but particularly with numbers, then a spreadsheet is useful. You might want to use it for accountancy work, for stock control, for catalogue items, even for suggesting lottery numbers. It's not quite such a *must-have* item nowadays as a word processor, but even if you used it only for converting Imperial measures to metric (why **convert**, for heaven's sake?) it could have a place in your software.

Accounts

Accounts programs are now a firm favourite for computer owners. A typical accounts program allows you to set up records for as many bank accounts as you need and keep track of what is happening to each of them as precisely as you bank does. You can ensure that standing orders and direct debits appear on the accounts and of course you can correct mistakes, something that is very difficult with accounts on paper.

Why do you want a PC?

Surprisingly few people have totally simple money affairs, with just one account, and an accounts program is ideal if you have, for example, a current account, a deposit account, and several building society accounts (if there are any building societies left by that time). If you juggle money between accounts and have more than one source of income (such as pensions) then the accounts program can be valuable because it provides the equivalent of a bank statement each time you run the program. A particularly valuable feature is that you can enter standing orders and direct debits and see the money deducted each month as the day for the debit comes around.

For more ambitious uses, accounts programs will give the value of a cash sum in several years time at a given interest rate, will warn you when payments are due on a loan, keep track of investments, show your expenditure broken down into categories that you want to use, and help you to plan. You can even keep more than one set of accounts, so that you can keep both household accounts and a small-business set of accounts in one file.

Games

Many computers are bought for games, particularly the modern multimedia games. Though it would be difficult to justify the cost of a computer for games alone, it is more reasonable if the computer is used for other purposes, and only the cost of the games software has to be considered. One of the enormous advantages of buying the PC type of computer, as distinct from other types and games consoles, is that the same PC machine can run both the serious applications and the games, with a huge choice of software.

Games come as junior or adult, useful or mind-rotting, and just about every level in between. If there are children in the house, the games need not be of the *zap the alien* type, but can be educational and useful. One publisher who specialises in particularly good educational software is **Dorling Kindersley** — though you will need a modern fast computer to do justice to some of their software.

More adult games are related to hobbies, so that you can run the signal box at Clapham Junction, fly a Boeing 747 or a Harrier, play chess at quite a strong level, study the stars even when the weather is poor, or fight the battle of Waterloo all over again but with your own strategy added on either side.

Games can be classed as activity, board games, puzzles, educational, simulations, and adventure. Unlike other types of program, in which you know pretty well what the program does, it's helpful to see a game program running before you buy it. Some adventure programs seem to be designed for dedicated crossword solvers and younger users will find them frustrating and boring.

Multimedia

Multimedia is one of the buzzwords of the nineties, and it means software that can produce text and pictures on the screen together with stereo sound from loudspeakers. Software of this type is always supplied on compact discs, and the CD must be inserted before the software can be used. This is unlike other software that is stored entirely inside the computer.

Multimedia is ideal for games, educational software and reference works. There are, for example, several excellent encyclopædias available, such as Microsoft Encarta (USA) and Hutchisons (UK). The differences between an encyclopædia in multimedia form and one in conventional form are enormous.

- The weight of a CD is negligible compared to that of 30 volumes of books.

Why do you want a PC?

- Topics can be found in a second or so using the CD version

- You have the attraction of colour pictures and, where appropriate, sound.

If you look up the name of a poet, for example, you can see text and an illustration and hear a poem spoken. Look up an animal and you have the information, the picture and the noise. Look up a musical work and you have its story, a picture of the composer and a piece of the sound. In addition, cross-references are easy, with no need to fumble through pages or find the right volume.

The use of multimedia allows for much more elaborate games to be designed, with pictures of stunning quality and (for fast computers) good animation. Alternatively, a complete set of simpler games can be placed on one disc, making it easy to change from one to another or even run more than one at a time.

The educational opportunities of multimedia have been well exploited, though the standard of software is variable. The discs from Dorling Kindersley are uniformly good, and several other suppliers have excellent material on offer. As for games, it's often useful to see what you are buying, and some suppliers are very helpful in this respect.

A few examples of multimedia software help to illustrate its possibilities. How about a route-finder for drivers? Type in where you start and where you want to finish (possibly adding where you want to call in), and a route is planned for you. The map appears, with your route highlighted. You can magnify parts of the map (zooming in) to see detail, look at town plans, see mileage figures, and even find the cost of the journey if you know the running costs per mile for your car.

If your interests are in gardening you can buy garden planners and garden problem-solving discs. You can plan meals, with recipes that show pictures and talk you through the tricky bits. You can check your health, find what that bird was that you saw last week, play Mastermind, or visit the art galleries of the world.

Internet

The Internet or World Wide Web has come to everyone's attention in the last few years. Joining the Internet means that you can use your telephone socket to connect your computer to others all over the world, and to exchange information.

At its best, this can mean access to information that is almost unobtainable elsewhere, discussions (at local phone rates) with computer users anywhere in the world, help with problems that you find impossible to solve. At its worst, it can mean endless waiting for phone lines to clear, frustration in trying to find the information you want, and hours spent in pointless arguments with some fanatic.

A great deal of money has been spent by advertisers in pushing the idea of the Internet, and though the subscription rates are low as compared to satellite or cable TV it is still an expensive hobby if you spend several hours each day — and remember that you are paying for the telephone time as well. Remember, however, that you have the choice of what you lookup on the Internet.

The main attraction of the Internet for the small-business user is *Email*, short for electronic mail, allowing instant communication with anyone who is also connected. You can, for example, send an A4 page of a letter to anywhere in the world in a fraction of a second, so that the cost is very low compared to that of postage, and if the recipient happens to be using his/her computer at the time, you might receive an equally fast reply. If not, the letter is stored until the recipient is ready for it. Unlike fax, there is no need to keep a machine switched on at all times — but you can send and receive fax using your computer if you want to, and you do not need to pay for any service provider.

What gives the Internet a bad name is the addiction that can develop to "surfing", looking for anything that catches your fancy and going from topic to topic for hours on end. The risk that was once voiced that young users could see unsuitable material is now less because the software can be arranged to make such material inaccessible — but you have to know how to do this. If you are worried about what your children can see, make sure that you know more about the system than they do.

Specialised uses

Though we have looked at some of the main ways that a computer can be of use, there are all sorts of minority uses. You can, for example, read written text or pictures into the computer using a (hardware) gadget called a *scanner*. This allows you to obtain text or pictures in computer file form, as if you had typed or drawn the work yourself. You can also get software that allows you to speak into a microphone and see the text appear on your screen, and save it as a word processor file. There is also software that will read text to you from a file.

If your interests are in illustration (graphics), the computer has become the normal way of producing pictures of all kinds. Computer aided drawing (CAD) software will create scale technical drawings for you with all the advantages of easy alteration and re-use of drawings. Picture editor software allows you to paint in colour, though it's difficult to produce the precise movements of a pencil or a brush. You can also start with a ready-made picture (perhaps a file of what is called *clipart*, or a photograph that has been scanned) and alter it until it suits your purpose.

Another minority interest is the editing of your video tapes, using the computer along with added hardware and software to control a video camera and an additional video recorder. You can now buy digital still cameras whose pictures are stored as computer files inside the camera. These files can be transferred to the PC, edited and printed (yes, you **can** now remove the tree that is growing out of mother's head). At the time of writing the quality of a print from a digital camera is not up to the level of a print from a cheap film camera, but the rate of progress is very fast, and remember that no film camera allows you to edit the photographs.

Music is well-served also. The computer can be used to control electronic instruments, using a form of connection called MIDI (musical instrument digital interconnection) so that you can control an orchestra of instruments and arrange your own music. Needless to say, you can then edit this music in the same way that the producer for a recording company would, and record it in digital form to be placed on a CD if you turn out to be a new musical genius.

Decision time

It's crunch time now. You should have some idea now whether you really want a computer and for what purposes. Perhaps only one of these uses appeals to you, perhaps most of them do. Even if only a few reasons are of interest that's good enough, and remember that new software is being written all the time, so that the capabilities of computers are continually increasing.

It's time now to look at what you need to buy, and perhaps what you don't need as well. Too many first-time buyers are sold a machine that is out of date, at an inflated price, or persuaded to buy a machine that offers much more than they need. There is at least some justification for buying a more capable machine because it will cope with more modern software and with your increasing requirements. If you want a less capable machine, the price should reflect the difference.

2 What machine?

If you look at any of the huge range of computing magazines you will be quite baffled at the number of suppliers and the huge variety of models that appear to be on offer. In fact, all PC machines are built to much the same pattern, just as all cars use the same pedal layout, so that you need not be too concerned about makes and models as long as the machine is a PC type and not one of the oddball variety that would separate you from the majority of computer users.

Looking at magazines, incidentally, is a superb way of getting to know values. Even if you don't speak the language, you can see what represents reasonable value at the time and what doesn't. Don't rely on advertisements in daily papers or displays in shops. Appendix A explains some of the most common abbreviations that you will find in advertisements.

You needn't be worried about brand names, either. The machines that carry the well-known names are not necessarily the best buys, and are often over-priced. All PC machines follow much the same pattern no matter who makes them, and the components are imported from the Far East and assembled here, in Europe, or elsewhere. Two machines made from the same collection of bits may carry price tags that are several hundred pounds different, so that there is nothing wrong in looking for a low price unless you are aiming to have the fastest or biggest machine in your road.

Another advantage of reading the magazines is that you start to recognise descriptions like 200MMX or 240P2 that indicate the type of *processor*. The processor is the heart of the computer, the silicon chip that does most of the work. Every few months, the design of processor chips advances and a more capable chip becomes available. Like a car, a new computer becomes out of date and less valuable as soon as you buy it and sometimes before. That doesn't stop anyone buying cars, and it shouldn't stop anyone buying computers.

- The point is that if it does what you want, it does not matter what comes after it or what value it might have second-hand.

The thing that **really** dates a computer is one particular type of software called the *operating system*. The modern machines all use an operating system called Windows 95 (or the later Windows 98 version). The previous generation could use one called Windows 3.1. The oldest machines can use only the system called MS-DOS (which later machines can also use if you want to use it). Only the more modern and fast machines, however, can take advantage of what Windows 95 and its successor Windows 98, can offer.

- One of the features of the PC type of machine is compatibility, so that even the most modern machines can still use the operating system and the software that was new in 1982. This is why the PC type of machine has been so popular — you don't have to throw away all your software when you buy a new PC.

Let's take a look now at where you can buy a computer and what choices you might make.

High-street shop

The 'high-street shop' means one of the electrical chain stores that can be found in almost every town in the UK. They stock refrigerators, washing machines, kettles, shavers, food processors — and computers. They don't specialise in computers, though there ought to be at least one member of staff who has specialised knowledge of computers.

You won't find bargain prices at these stores. At the rent and rates that these shops are paying it would be too much to expect bargains, but remember that you can take your time.

15

What machine?

You can see the machine in action, you can talk to someone about it, and if it gives trouble you can return it. You can buy on easy terms, though you have to remember that you can pay a lot extra if you do. Some shops will arrange some tuition as part of the price of the computer. These are all persuasive arguments for paying a little more than you might pay from other sellers.

Specialist shop

A specialist shop means a shop that sells computers and computer-related items and nothing else. Nowadays it is so easy to get hold of the bits that make up a computer that a lot of these shops assemble their own machines, and their prices are often very competitive. You can expect everyone in the shop to be knowledgeable and keen — though you might have to wait to be attended to.

You can also rely on the specialist computer shop to help you to upgrade the machine when something new comes along. This is much cheaper than buying a new computer, and if it's important to you to keep up to date this is the ideal way of doing it. Upgrading a computer that has been assembled locally from standard parts is often much cheaper than upgrading a 'famous name' machine which uses parts that were made to fit into a fancy casing.

Don't, however, be tempted by the books that a specialist shop stocks because they will usually be of US origin. These are usually expensive, and they deal with the US versions of hardware and software (which you won't have available in the UK).

Direct supplier

The advantages that a direct supplier can offer are competitive prices and in being up to date with the machines. Unlike the local computer shop, a direct supplier can order computer parts in thousands at low prices. Direct mail-order suppliers can assemble machines at lower cost, but their operation is not so vast that they need to clear a lot of old stock when something new comes along. Because they deal by mail, you have little chance of seeing what you buy in advance. However, if you have a credit card, buying can be very fast and simple, and if the advertisement has appeared in a reputable magazine you can reasonably expect the goods to be as they are described.

Direct suppliers include some of the best-known names in desktop computers, and there are a lot of names that you will never have heard of even if you have followed the progress of computing. Once again, magazines such as PC Answers can help because many of the mail order suppliers advertise in these magazines.

You can browse through the adverts looking at specifications and prices, and though it takes some time you will get to know which offers are genuinely good value for money. These will not necessarily be the cheapest or the dearest machines. For example, over the years the machines made by Dan Technology have consistently come out tops in reviews for good construction and quality parts, and Mesh is another top name for reliability at low price.

You also have a large choice of what comes with your computer. The word is 'bundled', and bundled software might be very important to you if you are buying a machine for the first time. It's not an advantage in paying a lower price for a machine if you have to spend several hundred pounds on software. Here again, the direct suppliers can get software at knock-down prices and pass the benefit to you. The biggest names in the bundled software business are the Granville group, using brand names Time, Colossus, and MJN. Most suppliers, however, will provide a large amount of bundled software.

Don't, however, be too dazzled by bundled software. It has to be useful to you to be worth anything, and the quoted retail prices are usually meaningless. If the bundled software is at least 75% useful to you, then go for it by all means. If it consists mainly of items that are of little use, disregard it. If you want to see approximate values, look at the adverts in the magazines for the same titles. Some bundled software consists of cut down versions, and you cannot tell until you open the packages and see give-away words like 'special edition' (or the letters SE). Ignore anyone that tells you that the bundled software is worth £350 or more — it will have cost the supplier less than a tenth of that amount.

New machine?

Should you buy a new machine? A lot depends on what your budget is, and one consideration to think about is that a new machine is often much better value for money than a used one. Currently, you can buy a very capable new machine for under £600, and you can be charged more than £200 for a machine that has had five years of hard life. If your budget is tight you have little choice, but there is no harm in waiting, because prices, if anything, tend to come down.

A new machine will always come with some sort of guarantee, and though computers are remarkably reliable there is a chance that you might need it. A second-hand machine might also come with a guarantee, but the price will reflect this.

The main point of a new machine is that it should be of the latest type. This doesn't always happen, and there are several machines currently on offer that would have looked rather old even a year ago — and a year is a long time in computing. How can you tell? It's all down to reading these magazines. For example, if you read in the magazines that all the better machines are coming with 64 Mb RAM, and the lower orders with 32 Mb RAM, you don't have to know your RAM from your CAD to see that a firm that offers 8Mb of RAM at a price higher than some of the 32 Mb models isn't exactly selling you a bargain.

You need a new machine if you want to run the most recent software, because on an older design such software will run dismally slowly. Speed isn't necessarily important at first, and many users are prepared to wait for hours for something to come over the Internet, but a machine that is too slow for its software will eventually infuriate you. This, incidentally, is another argument for seeing a machine working, using the software that you want, before you buy it.

Second-hand

Computers have a long working life, particularly the ancient models that had very few moving parts. Nowadays, computers hold their information on fast-spinning magnetic discs called *hard drives*, and these have a limited life. That life might be as low as four years, perhaps more than ten years — it depends on the number of hours for which the disc has been spinning, and if the computer was used for only a few hours per day there could still be a lot of life in a hard drive that had been working for eight years or more. In any case, a hard drive can be replaced, but this is something that adds to the cost of a computer, and you might have difficulty in finding a drive that would work on an old type of computer.

A year is a long time in computing, and it's most unlikely that a computer that was more than five years old would be up to your expectations. That does not make it useless, it's just that it would have to be used with software of its own time, not with modern software. It's not difficult to find such software because there is a vast quantity of it, and if the machine comes with suitable software that you can see running it might just fill your requirements as a first computer.

What machine?

In particular, if you want the machine for word processing a few letters, running some board games, the odd bit of accounts, then a second-hand machine can be very useful. As I said, it must match its software, and if it does and is easy to use, go for it. Make certain, however, that if you upgrade to a more modern machine later you will still be able to use either the same software, or more modern versions that can still read your files.

One point, however, is important. The price of a second hand computer should be low, **very low**. Thousands of capable machines were tipped into skips by NHS hospitals in the early nineties because they were being replaced by more modern versions and were thought then to have no value. If they had no value then, why should anyone charge over £200 for them now? You might perhaps read advertisements in the papers telling you that you can buy old computers for £35 and sell them for £250, and it's true that you can buy them very cheaply, though selling them depends on finding someone who hasn't read this book.

The most important factor is *where* you buy. Beware of the car boot sale — you don't know where the machine came from, you can't see it working and you may never see the supplier again. By contrast, a quick look through local advertisements will often uncover a 'computer mart' type of shop that deals mainly in second-hand computers. If the owner looks and sounds keen and knowledgeable there is a good chance of picking up a machine that is a genuine bargain. You might also find a good buy at a computer fair, but you need some experience to tell the wheat from the chaff. If you go to a computer fair to buy your first machine, take someone who has some experience with you, and don't be afraid to question prices and specifications. Computer fairs are often a way of disposing of items that can't be sold in any other way.

Old and slow

The lowest prices that you will find are for the older machines. Some are so old that you should not consider them unless you are interested in computing history. Whatever the name on the casing, the important way of classing a PC computer is by the processor type. Current models use some version of a processor called *Pentium*, but older models referred to the processor by numbers, all of which started with the digits 80. Processors are referred to using either the full name, such as 80486 or the last few digits, such as 486.

The 80486 machines are still respectably modern, and they will run a good range of software that was current in or around 1995. Because they are too slow for the latest software, they are now being discarded from offices, and should be a good buy if you can get one at a reasonable price — remember that the starting price for a new Pentium machine is now under £600

- Some machines use processors of other types that are described as being equivalent to Pentium or 80486. These are often perfectly capable machines, but they were cheaper when new, and should be very cheap second-hand. They can sometimes be difficult to upgrade.

Machines that use the older 80386 processor are getting decidedly long in the tooth now, and are much too slow for more modern software. They can use a good range of software that was available at the time, and which is still available nowadays, but you should not expect a machine in this class to cope with modern multimedia, even if it is fitted with a drive that will take CDs.

Machines that are described as 80286, or the even older 8080 or 8086 processors are really much too old. Unless you have an interest in older computers and are prepared to learn

21

What machine?

much more about controlling the machine you should steer clear of these. Even five years ago it was difficult to give them away. On the other hand, if you want to learn about the mysteries of MS-DOS and the programs that can be run using the system, a tenner or two might be well invested. The 80286 type of machine is much more capable than the older 8088 or 8086 types.

New and fast

The new and fast machines are all of the Pentium class, or fitted with processors that are of equivalent performance. The Pentium chips, however, are continually evolving and the most modern at the time of writing are Pentium-2 or the MMX Pentium designs. Older models carry numbers that range from 75 to 200, without the MMX letters or the −2 addition. By the time you read this there will be even faster versions available.

You have to ask yourself first if you need the fastest possible performance, and why. If you intend to use a lot of multimedia discs and you need to use the most up to date version of a word processor or DTP software, then you need a machine that is as fast as you can afford. If speed is not quite so important, spend less and have more available for other items, such as a printer.

- Remember, however, that if you opt for a cheaper and slower machine that you need to use software that matches the performance of the computer. In addition, prices of the faster Pentium machines are rapidly dropping to much the same levels as the slower types.

As it happens, most of the suppliers will offer such attractive prices on the not quite so fast or the not quite so new models that these are often the best buys. Remember that not many users need the fastest machine that is available, and some are working with computers that are, computer-wise, of the Jurassic period. Buying a new machine is always a finely balanced decision between what you long for and what you can afford, but there is no doubt that tomorrow's software will need a faster computer than today's.

What other bits?

If you go out to buy a computer you will probably come back with a printer also. If you only ever want to view text and pictures on the screen you can do without a printer, but if you want to use word processing, accounts, DTP and a whole range of useful programs then a printer is essential. Do without one at the start if you want, but remember that you will probably need it later.

A printer is not a luxury, but an expensive printer might be. Nowadays even a colour printer can be reasonably priced, but running costs might be another matter. If you are likely to generate a fair amount of printed work, then a good inkjet printer using a black ink cartridge is ideal. Look at models from Canon, Epson and Hewlett-Packard, and see them in action. Ask for an estimate of running costs, also, not forgetting the very expensive glossy paper that is needed if you want to reproduce photographs.

If you intend to go in for large amounts of printing and you need faster printing, a laser printer might be better for you. Again, the Hewlett-Packard and the Epson models are outstanding, but there are many others and though the running costs look high they are usually cheaper per page to run than an inkjet. Most laser printers are strictly black and white, and the few colour models are very costly and slow.

- Don't be afraid of second-hand old laser printers, particularly from Hewlett-Packard because the H-P Laserjet printers use toner (ink) cartridges and each time you put in a new cartridge you have replaced most of the parts that are likely to give problems. For the record, I am still using a Laserjet 2P, and the current model number is 6L.

23

What machine?

If you are not interested in the highest quality of printing you can easily find a second-hand printer of the dot-matrix type. The manufacturer to go for is *Epson*, though there are several others that are equally good for print quality. The main cost is of ribbons, and you can reduce this by using re-inking. Some machines use a very small ribbon that wears out rapidly, and one advantage of the older Epson models is that the ribbon is long and easy to re-ink.

Don't forget the cost of paper if you intend to do a large amount of printing. Laser printers can use the cheapest photo-copier paper, but some inkjets are fussy about the type of paper, and you may find that colour printing can amount to 10p per page if you want the best results.

Learning the language

In the course of looking at magazines and advertisements you will start to pick up some of the words and phrases (computerspeak) that are used to describe computers. You will also be more able to decide on which of two computers might be a better bargain, and, later on, what upgrading you might want or need.

To start with, a *byte* is a unit of stored data, and a useful way of thinking about it is that it is the amount of memory or disc space that is needed to store one character typed on the keyboard. For example, you would need eight bytes to store the word 'keyboard'. Not everything is stored in such a simple way, particularly things like numbers, pictures or sound, but the idea of one character per byte gives you something to grasp easily.

One byte is not exactly much, and even 1500 bytes (about the number of characters on an A4 page) is pretty small. To avoid using large numbers of zeros when we measure memory size or storage space, we use larger units. A kilobyte (Kbyte) is 1024 bytes, a megabyte (Mbyte) is 1024 Kbyte (which is 1048576 bytes), and a gigabyte (Gbyte) is

24

1024 Mbyte. For users who like to boast of such things, a terabyte (Tbyte) is 1024 Gbyte.

In the early days of the PC, a memory size of 64 Kbyte was thought to be enough for any imaginable purpose. Hard drives had not been invented, and a floppy disc of 360 Kbyte capacity afforded a luxurious amount of storage space. As our expectations have grown, the sizes of programs have also grown, and nowadays we expect a computer to have a memory capacity of at least 32 Mbyte (preferably 64 Mbyte), and a hard drive size that is around 2 Gbyte. We don't need the Tbyte unit yet, but some day we shall — just watch the advertisements.

The speed of a computer is not so simple to measure, but one way of comparing computers is to quote what is called the *clock speed* of the microprocessor chip. The clock signals are timing signals, and each action that the microprocessor can carry out will take a fixed number of clock signals, typically between 1 and 75. Each computer action is likely to need a large number of microprocessor actions (a bit like the Civil Service, really), so that if the computer is to work at a high speed, the clock rate has to be fast.

The units we use for clock speed are megahertz (MHz), meaning one million clock signals per second. At one time, a speed of 4.7 MHz was though to be daringly fast, but modern PCs work at much higher clock rates, typically around 200 MHz, with higher speeds on the way.

Though the clock speed is a good indication of the capability of a computer, it is only one of several factors. A computer with a 150 MHz clock speed might be faster to use than one with a 200 MHz clock if the 150 MHz machine had a fast-acting hard drive, a fast-acting graphics board, fast transfers of data and a fast CD-ROM.

The way that the computer is designed plays a large part in deciding how fast it can be used. Because of this, the

What machine?

reviews of computers that you see in magazines include a variety of tests using real software so that you can compare speeds on real tasks. You'll find that a computer that is faster on a word-processing test might be slower on a spreadsheet, or the other way round, and you have to decide for yourself what applications are of main interest to you.

The **screen size** is another measurement that is the source of confusion. In theory, a 14 inch screen should mean that the screen diagonal is of this size, but you may find that the diagonal that you can measure on the outside is nothing like this size. The 17 inch screen that I am using actually measures 15¾ inches diagonal, giving a picture of 12½ wide by 9¾ high. The manufacturers measure the diagonal of the tube itself, and because the edges of the tube are not visible when the monitor is in its casing, you cannot see the full diagonal.

You can find, then, that two monitors that are described as being of the same size need not measure precisely the same, and magazine reviews often quote the actual usable space. You should go for as large a screen as you can justify — at the time of writing most computers were using 15 inch (nominal) screen sizes rather than the 14 inch size, and 17 inch options are fairly common. You can expect that the 17 inch screen will eventually become a new standard, with 19 inch and 21 inch screens as the upgrade options.

Another quantity that you often find quoted is CD-ROM speed, but this does not use MHz units. The unit of speed for a CD is the average turning speed used for an ordinary sound CD. This is not constant — the sound CD spins faster when it is reading inner tracks than when it is reading outer tracks, so that quoting speeds in revolutions per minute, or centimetres of track read per second, do not mean very much.

The speed of a CD-ROM is quoted as, for example, 8x, meaning in this case that it revolves eight times faster than a sound CD. Speeds of up to 24x are now possible, but the fastest speeds are not necessarily an indication of better performance, though you will certainly find that speeds of less than 8x will not be acceptable for some multimedia software.

A fast CD-ROM needs to be assisted by fast transfer of data, and older computers cannot do this, so that using anything faster than 4x CD-ROM speed on an old machine is pointless. Modern computer can use a system called DMA (direct memory access) for speeding up the transfer of data from a CD-ROM, and this should be set up when you buy a new machine — ask the supplier about using DMA for both the hard drive and the CD-ROM drive.

Modem speeds are measured in terms of bits per second (bps), and with eight bits in each byte of data you can see that this is a measurement that is suited to the slower speeds of modems. For Internet use, a modem speed of around 16000 bps is considered an absolute minimum, and 33000 (or 33kbps) is better. At the time of writing, modems are available that can work at 56 kbps (56,000 bps), but there is no single agreed standard, so that you should avoid buying a modem of this speed unless you are certain that your Internet supplier can work with this type of modem.

- Modem suppliers often use the word *baud* to mean bits per second.

3 Opening the box

All right, you know how to open a box. Remember, though, that boxes these days are masterpieces of origami. If you open things in the right order, well and good, if not you will find yourself having to cut your way in with a chain-saw. You should try to keep the box in good condition in case you have to return the computer, or for when you move house.

Computers nowadays are usually packed in two large boxes. One box contains the main processing units of the computer (the computer case with keyboard and mouse), the other contains the monitor (display screen), and both boxes are heavy — if you intend to take them up stairs, get some help. The box that contains the monitor will usually have a *this way up* warning. This warning should be heeded, because like a colour TV, a monitor can be damaged by being placed with the screen surface downwards. The monitor contains a fine metal mesh, and if anything falls on to this mesh it can affect the picture at that point, causing perhaps a black dot or a dot that is always of the wrong colour.

The other box will contain the main computer in its metal case, the keyboard and mouse and any extras such as loudspeakers for a multimedia machine. The box will also contain any bundled software, manuals, an invoice and packing list, a guarantee, and packing materials.

If you are having a printer also, either as a separate item or as part of a package deal, this will almost certainly come in a third box. This box will contain the printer and it ought to contain a printer cable — but don't count on that. The printer box might also contain a spare ink supply (for an inkjet) or toner (for a laser printer) or ribbon (for a dot-matrix printer), but what you get very much depends on the manufacturer and the type of deal that you have negotiated.

- Always keep your packing along with the box in case you ever have to return the machine, or when the time comes to part with it or shift it to a new address.

Where do you put it?

You need to give some thought to where your computer will rest. Obviously you will want to use a table or desk, but do you know just how much space it will need? If you have bought a printer as well as the rest of the equipment, there may be too much to go on a table or a desk, and you might need an additional smaller table to hold the printer. Remember that if your computer is a multimedia type you will need to place one loudspeaker on each side of the monitor screen so that you can get true stereo sound.

- Take a look at the end of this chapter for some advice on desks or tables.

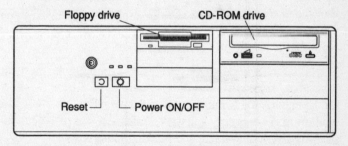

The most compact type of desktop machines (as distinct from portable computers) use a low-rise case, and the usual arrangement in the past has been to put the monitor on top of the casing. This was the usual arrangement when monitors were smaller and lighter, but putting a heavy monitor on top of the casing nowadays can dent the casing, particularly if the monitor is a large one. Get a piece of plywood the size of the top of the casing and use this to spread the load of the monitor, but keep it clear of any ventilation slots.

Opening the box

The trouble with this compact arrangement is that when the keyboard is at the right level for your hands, the screen is often too high for your eyes, causing strain on your neck. If you have plenty of desk or table space, you can put the monitor next to the casing, with the keyboard in front of the monitor. This is much less tiring to use, and the cables that are supplied are usually long enough to permit this.

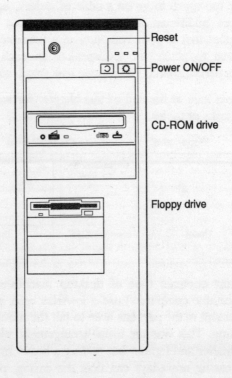

Reset

Power ON/OFF

CD-ROM drive

Floppy drive

The mini-tower casing (and its larger relatives, midi-tower and full tower) is often a much easier way of arranging the items when a larger screen (15 inches or more) is used. The computer casing is typically 39 cm (15 ½ inches) high, 21 cm (8 ¼ inches) wide and 41 cm (16 inches) deep, so that it takes up less desk space, and it is placed either on the desktop or (particularly for the larger tower units) under the desk.

- Do not place loudspeakers too near the monitor screen. Most small loudspeakers do not cause any noticeable distortion of the picture if they are taken close to the monitor, but some do, and in any case you will get better stereo effect if the loudspeakers are well separated. Both loudspeakers should face you as you sit at the keyboard — don't have one facing you and the other pointing sideways. Try to place the loudspeakers at least one foot from the monitor.

Space is just one aspect of siting a computer. In an ideal world, our houses would be built like some new US houses, with a separate computer room. That's unlikely, but if you have a modern house with a bedroom that is only just big enough to take a small bed, and no resident to worry about, that can make an ideal computer room. If you have to share the use of a room, things can become more difficult.

Ideally, you should position the computer so as to avoid the main perils of sunlight, dust, drinks and magnets. Sunlight on the screen makes it almost impossible to read on a bright day, and that same sunlight can also raise the temperature of the computer itself and any discs that you leave around to dangerous levels. Dust is a particular enemy of keyboards, so keep the cover on the keyboard when you are not using it. Need I say that the computer room should be a no-smoking area?

Heaters are another hazard. Keep any electric or gas heaters as far from the computer as possible. Even the conventional water-filled radiators need to be avoided because if cables

31

are draped across them the insulation of the cable is likely to perish, causing trouble sooner or later.

Coffee and other drinks are just as deadly. Few keyboards will work again after having a cup of coffee or a pint of bitter spilled over them, and all other liquids are just as destructive. It's not just damage to keyboards that can be serious, because discs can be damaged, and if you manage to spill liquids into the monitor or the main casing of the computer then you can only hope that your insurance will cover it.

Insurance is something that causes problems. In general, if the computer is used purely as a hobby item and not in connection with any business activity or as a money-earner, your household insurance will usually cover loss of the hardware. You need to notify your insurance company, particularly since a new machine with printer can easily be worth £1,500 or more, and this may be above the amount that most insurance companies allow for in the general set of household items.

- Be warned — if you make money, even at pin-money rates, using the computer, the amount you may be asked for insurance (assuming you can get **any** insurance) is more than would be needed for fully comprehensive cover on a £14,000 car. There is a large variation between companies, and you should shop around. Some companies simply refuse to insure a home computer that is used for any type of business, others charge prohibitive rates, but a few are prepared to quote on a much more reasonable basis, even for software or for portable computers.

Checking the components

When you take delivery of a new machine, the box usually has a sticker or contains a leaflet that lists the contents. In addition, the invoice that you get when you are asked to pay for the machine usually contains an inventory of this type.

As you unpack, check off each item in the inventory. You are, of course, gasping to get the machine connected up and running, but time spent checking the items will avoid the nuisance of finding later that there is something missing. The main thing to check, of course, is that this is the machine that you ordered, because most suppliers permit a dazzling range of basic machines and options.

Do not attempt to put each item into its final place as you unpack it. Connecting up is easier if you can get easy access to the back of the computer, and you want to take some time over connections if you have never done it before.

Connecting up

Whatever site you have chosen for your computer will need at least one mains socket and, if you want to use the Internet, one telephone socket. Computer equipment does not need a large amount of current, and plugs should be fitted with a 3A fuse, not the usual 13A one.

The more pressing problem is the number of connections that you might need to make. The main items of computer and monitor can be served with one plug, because the monitor mains cable is usually plugged into an outlet on the computer, using a special type of plug. A printer will need another socket, and it you have mains-powered loudspeakers they will need another socket.

If you have only one socket available, then you can buy a socket strip of four sockets and a plug, with enough cable to reach to where the computer is sited. That allows for as many plugs as most computer equipment will run to. You will need to switch off the main power to the socket strip after completing a computing session, to be certain that the other units (like loudspeakers) are switched off too.

Opening the box

If (**and only if**) you are competent and happy with carrying out electrical work, you can work with a two-socket strip. Use one socket for the main computer and one for the printer, and change the monitor cable for one with a three-pin conventional mains plug. Connect the special (Europlug) connector that was on the monitor to another three-way socket strip, and plug the monitor, the loudspeaker main supply and any other items into this set of sockets. That way, all the items that you use with the computer are switched on and off with the main computer itself. The exception is the printer, because you normally switch this on only when you need it, and off again when you have completed printing.

 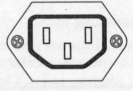

3-PIN MALE USED FOR POWER INPUT   3-PIN FEMALE USED FOR POWER OUT

- If the Europlug on the monitor cable cannot be dismantled, you can buy a detachable type from any Tandy or other electronics store. You will have to cut the old Europlug from the monitor cable so that you can fit an ordinary 3-pin plug.

If you have bought a computer that allows Internet connections, you will need a phone point. The cable that comes from the computer is usually long enough to reach a phone point on the same wall, but you can buy extension cables if you need to cover a longer distance.

- Note that if the computer contacts the Internet from a separate unit (an external modem), this unit will need a separate mains connection.

Now, with all the mains and telephone connections decided on, you can start connecting up the units of the computer system. You will need to have access to the back of the main computer casing, and to the back of the monitor. Check that you have all the loose cables you need before you start. For a normal set up these are:

- The mains cable that connects the computer to the mains socket

- The mains cable that connects between the computer mains outlet and the monitor mains input.

Other units have connecting cables that are permanently attached at one end, but if you have opted for specialised items, such as output to a TV/VCR, there will be some loose cables for these items. The mains cables are the only ones that carry dangerously high voltages, the others are data cables that carry only low-voltage signals.

Connect the mains cable that runs between the monitor and the main computer — this usually has a Euroconnector at each end, and can be fitted only one way round. The Euroconnector is used so that the exposed pins are never live to mains. Connect the video cable from the monitor to the video socket on the computer — this is the one with 3 rows of pins, fifteen pins in all.

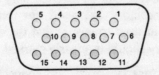

Like some of the other cables, the monitor data cable has securing screws on its plug. These may need a screwdriver or, more usually now, they may have knurled extensions that are easy to turn by hand. Screw these up, but only finger-tight. Their purpose is to prevent the plug from falling out,

Opening the box

and if you tighten them too much you will have problems when you try to remove them. The receptacle for these fasteners is itself only screwed into place, and it will come out with the fastener if you have over-tightened it. Beware of bending the monitor data cable too sharply.

Keyboard and mouse

The keyboard uses a small plug of the type called DIN. The more usual design is identical to the five-pin DIN type of plug that is used for audio equipment, and it plugs into a recessed socket. The position is clearly marked on some of the better-designed computers, but on others you will have to look for a hole in the back of the casing that conceals a socket.

Locating notch   DIN plug   PS/2 type

The keyboard plug has its pins arranged so that the plug can be fitted only one way round. If you try to insert the plug the wrong way you can damage the pins, so be gentle and check the fitting before you push the plug fully in. Some keyboards and computers use a miniature six-pin version of this plug, referred to as a PS/2 plug. This type of connector uses a socket that is mounted flush to the surface of the back panel of the casing, and also can be inserted only one way round. When PS/2 connectors are used for both mouse and keyboard, you will need to ensure that the correct socket is being used — they should be clearly marked.

The mouse can use a variety of connectors. The most common are the PS/2 miniature plug and socket, and the serial mouse plug. The serial plug uses nine pins and is of the same general shape (a D-type plug) as the monitor data plug, though with only two rows of pins. This is another connector that is usually secured by clamping screws, but the PS/2 plug is not, and more care needs to be taken with it.

Printers

Printer connectors are standard, and when you buy a printer you can be sure that it will connect with your computer. The printer cable uses two different connectors, one at the printer end and one at the computer end. Connect the cable into the printer first, using the end that has 36 connections that consist of copper strips laid on a sloping plastic support. The printer cable is always heavy and stiff, and must be firmly secured by its fixing screws at each end.

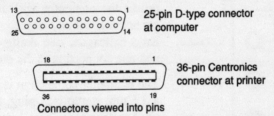

25-pin D-type connector at computer

36-pin Centronics connector at printer

Connectors viewed into pins

At the computer end of the cable, the plug is a D-type with 25 pins and this engages into the corresponding socket. Note that the computer will also have a *socket* that takes a 25-pin plug. This is a *serial* connector and is not used for the printer (they cannot be connected) unless you have a serial printer (so rare that we can forget about them).

More printer complaints can be traced to loose cables than any other cause, so be sure that the printer end in particular is well pushed home and secured. The design of the connector at the printer end is such that it only needs to loosen slightly to break the connections.

Other attachments – loudspeakers

If you are connecting up a multimedia system you will also have to connect the loudspeakers. Loudspeakers for multimedia are almost always of the type called *active*

37

Opening the box

loudspeakers, which means that they do not rely on the power of signals from the computer. One of the two active loudspeakers contains an amplifier, and has to be connected to the house mains supply. It also sends the amplified signal to the other loudspeaker.

When you connect up, one loudspeaker is placed further away from the computer, and this should be the loudspeaker that has only one cable emerging from it leading to the other loudspeaker. This is usually the left-hand loudspeaker (but check the instructions for your own loudspeakers), and if you reverse the position your stereo sound will be the wrong way round, with left and right reversed. The loudspeaker nearer the computer will use three connecting cables, one to its left-hand colleague, one mains supply, and one connection to the computer.

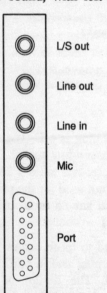

L/S out

Line out

Line in

Mic

Port

The computer connection is through a 3.5 mm stereo jack plug, and you need to take some care because the sound card in the computer will have three such sockets emerging from the back panel. One of these should be labelled as *loudspeakers out* or marked with the symbol for a loudspeaker. The other two are marked, in words, letters or symbols, as *microphone in* and *line in*.

• No harm will be done if you plug the loudspeaker cable into one of these other sockets, but you will hear nothing from the loudspeakers. You must be very careful not to use the loudspeaker socket for anything else such as a microphone.

The pile of booklets that will come with your computer should contain a drawing of the back of the sound card, with the positions of the sockets identified. The microphone input is used with a microphone when you want to record sound, use a phone-modem (to send voice messages across the Internet) or to use dictation software. The line input is used to accept signals from a cassette recorder, hi-fi system, or a separate CD player.

Modem

If your computer is capable of connection to the Internet, there will be other connections to make. Internet use is made possible by a device called a *modem*, and these come in two types of fitting, internal and external. New computers that come with a modem will almost certainly use an internal modem, so that the only connection that needs to be made is between the modem socket on the back panel and a standard BT telephone socket.

- One point about an internal modem is that you often cannot be sure when it has stopped using the phone line. This is one advantage of using an external modem, despite the extra cost and number of connections.

The external modem is a slim box that can sit on top of the computer or next to it. It will need a connection to the computer that uses one of the serial connectors. If you have a serial mouse connected to the 9-pin serial socket, the data cable of the external modem will have to be connected to the other (25-pin) serial socket. A similar connection will be used at the modem itself, and you will also need to connect the telephone line and a mains cable.

Manuals

A new machine will come with a set of booklets, each relating to some part of the computer such as sound card, main board (motherboard), video card, modem, monitor and so on. Some of these booklets are intended purely for the technical reader, and you will find out quickly enough which these are. Modem booklets in particular, contain long lists of codes that simply do not concern you and which you will never need to know, because the software carries out all the work.

You should keep all these manuals, however, because you may have to refer to them some day. In particular, if you ever want to upgrade your computer by adding more memory, you need to refer to the booklet concerning the main board or *motherboard* to find what you need to buy to carry out an upgrade.

If the machine has been correctly set up by the suppliers, you can ignore all advice about settings, particularly internal switches and jumpers. The jumpers are not of the woolly variety but lines of pins that can be connected by small clips, and all such connections should have been made for you. Check them if you want to, but do not alter any of them without asking the manufacturer, the supplier, or someone else who knows about the settings.

There will also be some software manuals, particularly if the machine comes with a large amount of bundled software. These manuals need rather more attention, because the software is your link to the computer and you need to be able to use it. It's best to work through each software manual with the computer running so that you can try things out.

Some software manuals can be ignored at first. There is usually a fairly thick manual concerning the sound software, and you do not need to pay much attention to this because it is directed more to people who want to use the computer as an electronic instrument or to control other electronic instruments. If you just want sound for using multimedia discs (as most users do) you can ignore this manual unless you suspect some fault in the sound system.

For other software, you will find that manuals are of variable quality. It's quite common, for example, to find what looks like clear advice (*type A: install and carry out the instructions that appear on screen*) that simply doesn't work, because the instructions were written concerning an earlier version. A lot of modern software dispenses with manuals, and relies on *Help* messages that can be shown on the screen. This is useful if you already know how to use the software, but isn't much help for the real beginner. Fortunately there are many books produced independently of the software manufacturers, but a lot of these are from the USA and are written around the US versions of software. Insist on books written and produced in the UK if you want to be able to use the UK version of software.

Second-hand computer installation

Installing a computer that you have bought second-hand is in some ways easy and in other ways more difficult than starting with a new machine. Over the course of a few years, manuals may have been lost, labels can fall off, and though the previous owner knew from experience where all the plugs fitted, you don't.

A old machine that is being sold as a surplus bargain by a firm such as Morgans will usually come with documents that will help you to get it going, and this is reflected in the price. Similarly, if you are buying directly from the previous user you can ensure that you have it all explained, and you can take notes and attach labels for yourself. It is more difficult if you have pulled a bargain offer from a pile of old machines at a computer exchange shop or at a computer fair.

One useful point to remember is that older machines are usually well-documented machines, and provided that you avoid the weird designs (often the ones that carry some famous name) you should find that the connections are of a standard variety. As I said earlier, there is nothing wrong in

Opening the box

buying a machine that carries an unfamiliar name, and it's often a positive advantage. If you want to convince yourself, look in the magazines for the cost of memory for ordinary machines and for famous-name machines. The difference is what you pay for that nameplate, not for superior design, longer life or greater reliability.

Caring for your PC

Once you have your first computer up and running (or about to run) you need to know a few tips that help to keep it in good condition. The most important of these concern the hard drive that stores all of the programs and (eventually) all of your own data files. The hard drive consists of a set of discs (or platters) that are spinning at a high speed and have read/write heads held very close to each surface. The read/write heads are like miniature pickups, and they must be held very close to the surface of a platter without ever touching it.

- If you jolt, bump, move, or drop the main computer box while the hard drive is working you will almost certainly cause damage to the platters. This cannot be repaired and because the hard drive is a sealed unit the only remedy is to replace the whole drive. All the information that is contains will be lost unless you possess or have made backup copies.

This sounds as if the whole thing is just too delicate to work with, but it's not as bad as all that. The hard drive will withstand a lot of bashing about when it is **not** working, so that you can shift your computer around when it is switched off. Even when the computer is switched on, kicking the leg of the desk or table accidentally will not necessarily do any damage — it all depends on how hard you thump it. It would, however, be very foolish to try to move the computer while it was working.

You see many advertisements for computer desks, and a lot of them look very flimsy. A modern desktop computer is heavy and it needs a sturdy desk or table. An old kitchen table that is good enough for rolling out pastry is probably good enough to take a computer (but remove the pastry first). The ideal site is a really solid plain old desk, and these can sometimes be found in junk shops because the antiques hunters are looking for the leather-topped type. The main thing is that if you bang into such a desk you will not shift it or wobble it, and your computer will not be affected.

- The other very important point about your hard drive is that you must never, **never,** switch off the computer while the hard drive is working. You will know when the hard drive is working by the light (activity light) that appears on the front panel of the computer, and you should check with the manual for your computer to find which light this is.

Windows 95 and 98 require you to go through a switch-down process by clicking a shut down option and waiting for a message that tells you when you can switch off. Always use this procedure, because if you switch off while the hard drive is working you will quite certainly lose some information. You might not notice the effect for some time, but something, somewhere, will not be as it ought to be.

- Always keep backups, because this ensures that if the worst happens and you lose files, you will have spare copies so that you can restore the data on your hard drive. Even if you don't know how to restore the files, having the backups will allow someone else to do the work.

- Windows includes two utility programs that are used to check your hard drive and keep it at peak performance. The SCANDISK program will check the drive for errors and ensure that any bad portions of the drive

43

remain unused. The DEFRAG program will rearrange the files on the drive so that they can be read and written quickly.

The most vulnerable parts of your computer system are the floppy discs, because these are not sealed and they live most of their life outside the computer. You will use floppies mainly as backups, so storage is particularly important. You should store floppies in a cool place, away from direct sunlight and clear of hot pipes, radiators or other heat sources. You must also keep them well away from loudspeakers and anything else that contains magnets. If your floppies are in plastic envelopes, keep them there until you need them. Never pull the shutter back and touch the magnetic surface of a floppy.

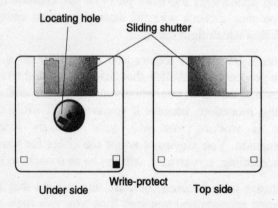

Locating hole   Sliding shutter

Under side   Write-protect   Top side

Each floppy should be labelled, and when you buy a pack of new floppies it will contain a set of paper labels. You should not write on these labels when they are stuck to the floppy unless you use a felt-tip pen. Preferably, you should write the label and then stick it to the top side of the floppy.

Remember that if a floppy contains particularly important data you can write-protect it, meaning that when you put it into the computer it can be read but the computer cannot alter its stored data. This is done by sliding the little cover plate so that you can see through the hole at one side of the disc.

Programs and data on CD-ROM are much more secure, but you should try to avoid touching the recorded side of the CD (opposite the label). Any dust and/or fingerprints should be wiped off using a soft clean cloth and wiping across the tracks, that is, from centre to edge.

The other parts of your computer that need some care are the keyboard and mouse, and the main point of concern is to keep them clean. Always replace the keyboard cover when the computer is not in use, so that dust does not settle between the keys. If you use a mouse mat, turn it over or cover it when it is not in use.

4 Software

Software is what makes a computer useful, just as records make a gramophone useful and books make a library useful. A dead piece of machinery becomes a word processor, a bookkeeper, a designer, a painter, a music editor; all because of the software that you use.

At one time, a desktop computer would be supplied with no additional software. It had, built into it, the software that allowed you to write programs for yourself, and that's why books about computers in the past (from around 1978 to 1986) were so concerned with programming. Nowadays no-one is expected to do any programming, only to use the vast set of software that can be run on the PC type of computer.

At one time, all software for the PC machine was run using a system called MS-DOS, an *operating system*. To run a program, you had to insert a disc (or use the hard drive), type the program name, and press the *Return* key (marked with a hooked arrow). Another key marked *Enter* could be used in place of the return key. Each action was carried out by typing a command word, perhaps some other information, and pressing the *Return* or *Enter* key. Programs that require these MS-DOS commands are said to *run under DOS*.

All PC machines can use this system, because the MS-DOS operating system is still present in your PC, old or new. The more recent computers, however, use an additional system called *Windows* that make it all easier. Files are represented by miniature pictures called icons, and there is a pointer on the screen that can be moved by moving the mouse. Actions are carried out by moving this pointer and clicking the left-hand button on the mouse. For example, to run a program, you place the screen pointer over its icon and click twice in quick succession (a double-click). To copy a file, you place the pointer over the icon, hold down the mouse button and move the mouse so that the program icon appears in a different place among other files. This action is called *dragging*.

The use of Windows means that you do not have to type names or remember commands. More importantly, it ensures that once you are accustomed to these clicking and dragging actions you will use the same actions on any program. You do not need to learn any new actions when you buy a new program, providing that the program *runs under Windows*. All the programs that are supplied with a new computer will use Windows, and the version of Windows that will be supplied will be the most recent, currently Windows 95 or Windows 98. The previous Windows version was 3.1, and if you are offered a computer that uses the older version Windows 3.0 you should think twice, because though you can get an upgrade to Windows 3.1, the machine itself might not be good enough for your purposes.

Windows makes use of MS-DOS; it is a simpler way of issuing the MS-DOS commands. Because it's indirect, it needs a computer with more memory, more hard-drive space, and faster action than one that uses only MS-DOS directly. Before Windows, we thought that a computer with a memory of 640 Kbyte was pretty well equipped. Nowadays, we want fifty times that amount, and the demands for hard drive space and speed have increased. That's the price you pay for convenience, simplicity and more features on your software.

Your first PC should certainly use Windows — apart from anything else, a machine that is not equipped with Windows will be too old to contemplate unless it is at a knock-down price and with lots of useful software and manuals. A new computer will come with Windows installed. Currently this will be the version called Windows 95, but in the lifetime of this book the later version, Windows 98, will be used. If you buy a second-hand bargain, you may find Windows 3.1

Software

installed, and you can learn a lot using this version — you may even find some actions simpler. You will not, however, be able to use any of the modern software that has been written for Windows 95 and Windows 98.

Pre-loaded software

There are few new computers nowadays that are not supplied with software preloaded. That will certainly mean Windows 95 or 98, and it will also usually include other software such as office packages (word processor, spreadsheet, presentation, accounts, etc.), multimedia and games.

Preloaded software should be ready to run, so that you can click and go on any of it. The original discs should also be supplied, however. These discs prove that you are entitled to the software, they may contain a registration number and a phone number to call to register your right to the software. Without the original discs your right to the programs can be challenged, and if anything happens to delete or corrupt the software on your hard drive you have no way of replacing it.

In the past, manufacturers have often filled most of the hard drive with this pre-loaded software, leaving very little for you unless you removed some of the preloaded stuff. Nowadays suppliers are more reasonable and hard drives are of greater capacity.

What can you expect? One very popular pre-loaded item is Lotus Smartsuite which, as the name suggests, is a set of office programs that includes the very useful *Word Pro* word processing program. Other suppliers preload the Microsoft program suite called *Works*, and some offer the excellent book-keeping program called *Quicken*. The choice is yours, but you should concentrate on how much of a bargain the computer itself is rather than on the preloaded software. Obviously you need some software to get started, but provided that you have Windows and some software that is useful to you the rest is not so important.

Other bundles

In addition to the software that is bundled and pre-loaded, many suppliers will also bundle discs for other software which is not loaded, and which you can load or not as you choose. Multimedia and games software usually falls into this category.

This software has to be treated with some care. Some of it may be useful, some of it may be good, but it doesn't follow that the useful stuff is good or the good stuff useful. Some of the offerings may be cut-down versions of software that sells for quite a high price, and this price may even be quoted to show you what a bargain you are getting. A few examples are politely described by those in the know as *crippleware*, meaning that they are of very little use. As an example, I have a program that has to be totally transferred to the hard drive to work at all, and which occupies ten times the amount of space of the usual program on CD. Added to that, the instructions for loading it are incorrect. Who needs bargains like these?

Some of these *thrown-in* programs are good. Perhaps the program is about to appear in a new version and the manufacturer is disposing of the older ones. Whatever the reason, you can bet that the computer supplier probably paid £2 or less per disc for them, and you can ignore any references to retail prices. Remember that magazines priced at £2.20 to £3.50 come with CDs attached, so it's obvious that these CDs did not cost a lot to the supplier of the magazine.

How to see what you've got

How do you check that you have the pre-loaded software, or that a second-hand computer contains the programs that the seller claims? It's most unlikely that software that should have been preloaded will be missing, but the contents of a second-hand machine are more dubious. Before we can answer this point you need to know more about how programs are stored on the hard drive and how Windows will list them for you.

A program very seldom consists of just one stored file. It is much more likely to be a collection of files, one of which will be the main program file with others used as supplements. File names follow a standard pattern that consists of a main name followed by an extension of up to three letters, separated by a dot. Using Windows 95, the name can contain up to 255 letters, but many names still use the older MS-DOS limit of up to 8 letters or digits. For example, a file might be called mywords.doc — the main name is *mywords* and the extension is *doc* (usually meaning that this file was created by a word processor compatible with Microsoft Word).

The main file of a program will use the extension letters of *exe* (sometimes *com* for short programs), so that if, for example, you had a program called *scribe*, its main file would be called *scribe.exe*. Your Windows system should be set so that it reveals these extensions — an option is to hide them so that only the main name shows. Along with this main *exe* file there will be supplementary files, several of which are likely to use the *dll* extension. This is short for dynamic link library, a collection of program codes that the main program can call upon when needed.

If every program that you used placed all of its files on to the hard drive without some attempt to group the files it would be very difficult to find what files belonged to what program. Remember that a reasonably well filled hard drive might contain more than 2,000 files. The method that is used to group files together makes use of *folders*. A folder has a name, like a file, but it is used to group files. You might, for example have a folder called *words* that contained *scribe.exe* and all the other files of this (imaginary) word processor.

This use of folders makes it much easier to locate all the parts of a program, and it also avoids overloading the hard drive, because there is a limit to how many file names can be used directly in a hard drive. If the files are arranged in folders, the only limit to the number of files that you can have is the storage capacity of the hard drive, rather than a much smaller number of names that can be used.

Another advantage of using folders is that you can have files that bear the same name, but located in different folders. If, for example, you save a file called *mystuff.doc* into a folder that already contains a file of precisely this name, the new files replaces the older one. If you save your new *mystuff.doc* into a different folder that does not already contain a file of that name, the older version is unaffected.

Windows 95 uses a program called Windows Explorer to display and find your programs and files. To use Explorer, do this:

1. Click on the Start button at the bottom left-hand corner of the screen, or press one of the keys with the Microsoft flag (next to Alt and Alt Gr on some keyboards).

2. Move the pointer with the mouse so that it rests on the word *Programs*, and a new set of names will appear to the right.

3. *Windows Explorer* will be at or near the bottom of this set. Click (once) on this name to start Explorer running.

When Explorer is on screen, it appears as two columns. The left-hand column lists the folders. Some folders contain other folders, and this is indicated by a box with a + sign to the left of the folder icon: Click on a folder icon or name to see its contents list in the right-hand side of the Explorer display. When a folder contains other folders, these will also

51

Software

appear in the contents list, and you can recognise them by the folder icon. Other files, the program files, will use different icons

You will see your bundled software in the form of folders, usually with other folders enclosed so that the [+] sign will appear. You can check that you have a folder that corresponds to each bundled item.

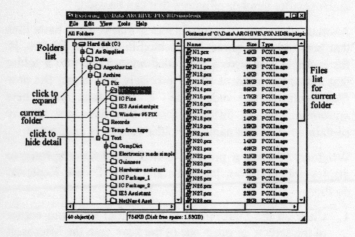

- Explorer allows you to delete folders and all their contents. Do not do this unless you know for certain that there is nothing in a folder that you want. There will be several folders whose names you do not recognise, but do not be tempted to delete them just because of that. They may contain files that are essential to other programs.

- There are usually several folders that carry communications programs for the Internet, some with offers of free use for a trial period. Remember that if you take up these offers, you will be asked for credit-

52

card details, and you will nccd to ensure that you cancel a service in time if you are not to incur charges.

- If you have bought an old computer that uses Windows 3.1, the File Manager program carries out the actions of displaying files and folders — the word *directory* was used for what we now call a folder.

How to add software

You can add software, either from the set of discs that has been included, or from discs that you buy or obtain from magazine covers. These can be the 3½ inch floppy discs or the larger CD-ROM type. The floppy is useful for short programs, but large programs and sets of programs have to be distributed on CD-ROM because so many floppy discs (typically 30 or more) would be needed for the same amount of data.

There are two main ways of adding the software, and you need to be guided by the instructions on the disc. If you are using a CD-ROM you need to know the reference letter for the CD-ROM drive. It is usually **D** for a computer with one hard drive, but on some large machines it might be **E** or **F**. The floppy drive is always lettered as **A**, and the (main) hard drive as **C**.

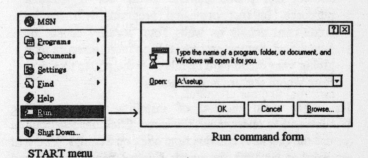

START menu

Run command form

The installation starts with placing the disc (or the first disc of a set of floppies) into the drive. Click on the *Start* button or press the Microsoft flag key if you have one. Now click on the word *Run*, and in the space that appears, type the instruction for starting installation. This will be the drive and name of the installation program.

The program that arranges a folder on your hard drive and copies the files will have a name that is either **install.exe** or **setup.exe**. So that the correct drive is used you must precede this by typing the drive name, a colon and a backslash. Typically you might use:

a:\install   or   a:\setup   to install from the floppy drive

or

d:\install   or   d:\setup   to install from the CD-ROM drive.

When you have typed the command into the Run space, click on the OK box. Once this has been done, the process is usually automatic. You might be asked if you approve of the name for the folder that will be created, but there is no need to type a different name unless there is already a folder of the same name in use. This is not very likely, so that you can simply move the mouse pointer over the OK box and continue.

• Some programs will require you to type in your name, address and phone number details for registration purposes. Internet provision programs will require credit-card details as well. Total security cannot be guaranteed, but the procedure is no more insecure than giving your credit card details over the phone to a firm from whom you are buying goods.

The other main method of installing programs using Windows 95 is really much the same. Click the *Start* button (or use the flag key) and this time click on Settings. You will see another list with the words Control Panel, Printer and Taskbar. Click on *Control Panel*. When the Control Panel appears, **double-**click on *Add/Remove Programs*, and then on *Install/Uninstall*. Follow the instructions, and the installation program will be found and used automatically with no need to type anything.

The procedure using Windows 3.1 is very similar to the first method. The *Program Manager* window contains a menu item called *File*, and you click on this and then on the *Run* item in the list. From then on you type the drive and installation name such as a:\install and click on the OK button or press the Return key to start the action.

- You should buy a good beginners' book that illustrates the Windows actions. Try one from the *Babani* set or one of the *Made Simple* series. Avoid books of US origin that assume that you are a retarded teenager.

Formatting floppies

Floppy discs do not hold a lot of information, but just a few might hold all that you create in a year, so it's important to be able to use them, particularly for backup (see Chapter 5). The important thing to know is that you cannot just buy a floppy disc, put it in the drive and then save your files on it. A new floppy disc has to be formatted, a process that gets it ready for use.

Formatting is easy using Windows 95. Put the disc into the floppy drive and do this:

1   Click on the *Start* button, or use the flag key, and move the pointer to *Programs*. On the list that appears at the side, click on *Windows Explorer*.

- Note that if you used Windows Explorer the last time you used the computer, and did not shut it down, it will restart automatically.

2   Click on the name near the top of the folders list, just under *Desktop*. This is usually called *My Computer*, or it may carry the maker's name for your computer.

3   The list at the right will now show a few names. One of
    these will be 3½ floppy (A:). Click on this name.

4   Now click the *File* menu, and on the list that appears,
    click *Format*.

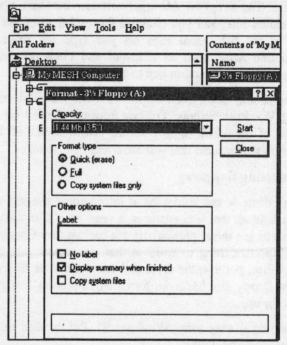

5   On the panel that now appears over the Explorer display,
    click the box labelled *Full* to format a new disc. The
    Quick option can be used for a disc that has been used
    before, such as an unwanted disc bundled with a
    magazine.

6   Wait until the action is finished. You will be offered the
    choice of formatting another disc, and you can do this if
    you have a batch of new floppies to format.

• Never, **never**, attempt to format your hard drive
  because this will wipe all the files from it. An expert

can cope with this and recover files, but you aren't an expert — yet.

Keep your formatted floppies separate from the unformatted ones, and stick a label on them. There is provision for a *label* in the formatting process, but this is a file name and you cannot see it until you insert the floppy in the drive and start it.

If you are going to subscribe to magazines, it's often better to take the (cheaper) floppy disc option, because if the programs that come on each disc are of no interest to you (and some of them are not likely to be of much interest to anyone) you can use the Quick Format option on these discs. It's the cheapest way of collecting floppies. If you take the CD option you cannot make use of the CDs for your own purposes (unless you know some way of recycling them into plant-pots).

5 Backing up

Backing up means making copies of valuable files, and it's something that becomes more important as you make more use of your computer. When you start using your first computer, all the files have either been loaded in advance or you install them yourself from CD-ROM or other discs. You don't really need any backups at that stage, though you will be advised to make backups of any files that were provided on floppy discs.

What makes backing up more important later is that the hard drive of your computer is in use all the time the computer is switched on, and that might be all day. It's true that on some modern computers the hard drive is switched off when you have not used the keyboard for several minutes, but the action of starting the drive up again also contributes to wear and tear. The hard drive is a mechanical device and all mechanical devices will wear out in time; they all have a limited life. Your hard drive isn't going to give up today or tomorrow, and if it did the guarantee would take care of most of the cost (such as £180 for a new drive and the same again for fitting it if you don't do it yourself).

Some day, though, the hard drive **will** give up. The process may be slow, indicated by niggling faults, or it may be quite sudden. It isn't necessarily spectacular; quite often all you know is that you switched on and nothing happened, no hard drive noise, none of the usual starting messages. Sometimes it might not be a hard drive failure, just a problem with software, but the effect is just the same. This calls for backup.

There are two types of items that you really, **really**, must back up. One is the set of essential files that will start up the computer. These are the equivalent of a skeleton crew, and they let you start in MS-DOS so that you can use the utility programs that, with luck will repair some types of hard drive faults. This type of backup, called a Startup disc or rescue disc, is not useful if the hard drive has completely failed and is not spinning, but it is very useful if hard drive errors are reported or if the hard drive spins but does not start MS-DOS or windows.

- You might not be able to use the Startup disc for yourself in an emergency, but the fact that you have one does at least allow a more experienced user to get things going again for you.

The other concerns your most valuable files. These are not files of programs that were preinstalled or bundled. They are not files that came on discs that you bought, even if you paid several hundred pounds for them. They are the files that you have created for yourself using your programs.

Think of it this way. Perhaps you use a word processor program and an accounts program. In the course of a year you will have typed a lot of words into the word processor. There will be files of all your letters, names and addresses of everyone you know, all sorts of documents that you have created. The accounts program will have created file records of all the money that has come into and gone out of your bank accounts, all your standing orders and direct debits, when payments start and end, perhaps tables that are essential for your tax return.

All this has taken you hours of work, and though you might have copies on paper somewhere it would take many more hours to type everything in again. Would you ever get it just as it was? What is all that time worth? These are the really valuable files, and though you can insure a computer at extortionate rates, you simply cannot insure your own data files, mainly because they are continually changing and being added to. For peace of mind, you need to back them up.

Backing up

Of course if you use a computer for multimedia displays and games, there will be very few, if any, files of data to back up, and you might very reasonably ignore this point. You should not ignore the creation of a Startup disc, however.

Startup disc

A Startup disc can be made easily using Windows 95. You will need a 3½ inch floppy that has been formatted, see Chapter 4. Make sure that you use a disc that has nothing valuable saved on it, because anything on the disc will be wiped when you create the Startup files. Put this floppy into the floppy drive and go through the following routine:

1   Click the *Start* button of Windows 95, or use the Flag key if you have them on your keyboard.

2   Move the pointer to *Settings*, and on the list at the side, click on *Control Panel*.

3   Double-click on *Add/Remove Programs*.

4   Click on *System Disk*.

From then on, obey the instructions that appear on the screen. Once the disc has been created, label it and store it in a safe place, somewhere that is cool, dry and well away from magnets.

Making a Startup disc is like insurance — it's better to have it and not need it than to need it and not have it. Personally, I have never needed one, but that doesn't mean I never will. As you get to know more about computing you might get careless about this type of backup, and that's just the time when you get that nasty feeling that comes when you realise that you switched on fifteen minutes ago and nothing has happened.

• If you have bought an old computer with Windows 3.1, insist on some form of Startup floppy disc, because making one for yourself is not so easy as it is for

Windows 95 and later versions. The disc should contain some essential MS-DOS files, and will be enough to make recovery possible. Once again, that does not necessarily mean that you could do the recovery, but it makes it possible for a more experienced user. A hard drive on a new machine is so reliable that you are likely to be pretty experienced by the time you encounter a failure, but a hard drive on an older machine might have a lot of miles on the clock.

Copying floppy discs

You are often advised to make copies of the floppy discs that are used to distribute programs. This is rather old-fashioned advice, going back to the days when computers did not have hard drives. In these days, floppy discs were used intensively, and to run a program you had first to load it from its floppy disc or discs. Because the disc was used so intensively, it needed backing up by copying its files to a floppy that was not used at all, just stored in a safe place.

Nowadays any program that came to you on a floppy disc and is useful will have been placed on the hard drive. That means the files will always be used from the hard drive, and the floppy will never be used again unless something happens to the copy on the hard drive. This disc is its own backup, and it can be stored in a safe place. You might, however, want to make another backup just for peace of mind, particularly if the program is a valuable never-to-be-repeated one.

Another point is that some programs on floppy discs invite you to make copies and circulate them to your friends. This is all very well if the program came from a reputable source, but if it was handed to you by someone you don't know well, avoid it. Such a disc might contain a virus that could affect all the files on your hard drive. There are methods of

61

Backing up

checking floppies for virus infection, but it's easier to avoid using the floppy in the first place.

If the floppy is genuine, such as one that was attached to a magazine you bought new, you might want to copy it. Do not, on any account, pass on or sell files that you have copied from floppies that are copyright, because this can land you into trouble. You are allowed to make backups, but for your own use only.

To make the copy, using Windows 95, put the floppy into its drive and:

1   Start *Windows Explorer* if it is not already running — see earlier for details.

2   Click on the *My Computer* (or equivalent) name near the top of the folders list.

3   Click on the name *3½ floppy (A:)* in the files list.

4   Click on the *File* menu, and on the item called *Copy Disk*.

5   Obey the screen instructions, particularly when you are asked to take out the floppy and put in a blank formatted floppy. Your copy will be made on this floppy.

• At the moment, you can make backups using writeable CD-ROM discs, but these discs are not compatible with the ordinary type of CD-ROM. In the lifetime of this book, however, machines fitted with read/write CD-ROM drives will become available.

Saving and backing up your data

As I noted earlier, your own data is by far the most valuable set of files that you have, and it's essential to back up this data, because if it is lost you cannot go out and buy another set.

When you are starting up, you are not likely to generate much data for yourself, and one or more floppies will be enough to keep as backups. As your use of the computer expands, however, you are likely to need more and more backup, and there may come a time when you are looking at a collection of 30 or more floppies containing your data. When that time comes you need to think more seriously about backup.

The simplest method of backing up is to copy each of your data files to one or more floppies. If you use a distinctive name for each of your files, you can copy them all to one floppy. In time you might need more than one, but the principle is the same — you are simply making file copies.

If you are using Windows 95, you need to run Windows Explorer, and it's a good idea never to close Explorer. That way, it will be loaded ready to work for you next time you start Windows. If you are using an older machine that runs Windows 3,1, then start File Manager.

Put a formatted blank floppy into its drive. Using Windows 95 Explorer, locate the folder that contains your data files, and then:

1　Select the files that you want to save. If they are in a column, click on the first one, hold down the Shift key and click on the last one. The files will appear in reversed colours, usually white letters on a black background. Another method is to select one file by clicking, then hold down the Ctrl key and click on any others you want to use — this is better if the files are scattered around.

2　Click the File menu name, and move the pointer to Send To. The list that appear will contain 3½ floppy (A). Click on this to copy all of the files to the floppy.

3　If you have more data files in another folder, save them in the same way.

Backing up

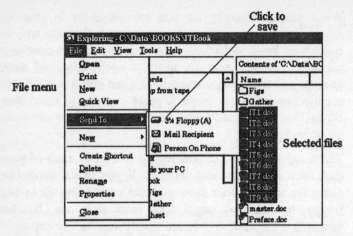

File menu

Click to save

Selected files

- If you are using Windows 3.1 and File Manager, use one side of the display for your folder and the other for the floppy and drag your selected files from one to the other.

When the time comes that you need more than one floppy to hold all of your data files you may need to split them into groups. The best method is to use separate folders, with each folder containing enough files to store comfortably in one floppy. A floppy will hold about 1.4 Mbyte, and when you use Explorer the status line at the bottom of the screen will show the amount of space needed for the files you have selected.

Eventually, making backups may need so many floppies that it becomes cumbersome. By that time, you will be experienced with the use of Windows, and you will be able to use the Windows Backup program. This can code your files so that many more will fit on each floppy, the equivalent of 4 Mbyte or more. If you need large amounts of backup for business purposes, then the best method is to add a tape backup drive to your computer.

6 Printers

A printer is often part of a package deal when you buy a new computer, and is equally likely to be part of a second-hand deal. If your use of the computer is confined to games and looking at multimedia displays, then a printer is not a first priority.

A printer starts to become important if you use, for example, word processing or accounts programs. There is not much sense in typing a letter on the screen and not being able to print it on paper, and I don't think you would cut much ice with the Tax Inspector if you tried to present your accounts on screen.

In addition, as you explore the abilities of your first computer, you will see Help notes and all sorts of advice in files that carry the extension letters of TXT. Some of these are too long to display on one screen, and it would take a long time to make notes about them, so that printing them is the best way of extracting the information.

We have seen already that there are three main types of printers, inkjet, laser and dot matrix. Of these, a new computer that comes with a printer will almost certainly feature an ink-jet model. An older computer might be packaged with a dot matrix printer. You should consider a laser printer only if you need to turn out professional work, such as camera-ready copy for books.

Using the printer

The printer needs to be close to the computer, because printer cables are relatively short, 2 metres at the most. This is not because the makers are stingy with their cables, it's because the cable just has to be short if the signals on it are not to become jumbled — there are eight signals going along the cable for each printed character. If you absolutely must have a longer printer cable, you can buy one that incorporates an amplifier that will boost and separate the signals, but it's much easier and cheaper simply to keep the printer next to the computer.

We have looked at the fitting of the printer cable already, and the advice to remember is that the plug at the printer end is the one that needs attention — it must be pushed completely home and secured. Try to avoid any strain on this or the other plug, and do not try to bend the printer cable through a sharp angle.

Simply connecting a printer to the computer and to a mains power supply does not ensure that the printer will print anything. Many printers allow you to print a test sheet which will show that the printer itself is working, but it does not test that it can print anything *from the computer*. Like every other computer action, printing depends on software, and the type of program that is used to control a printer (or the mouse, monitor, and other items) is called a *driver*.

Each different model of printer needs its own driver software to allow the special features of that printer to be used. There are some families of printers in which all of the models in the family can use the same driver, but you still have to install the driver. If the printer has come as part of the package, ask if the driver for Windows is installed. If it is, you have nothing to do but print whatever you want to print, and we'll look at that later.

If you have bought the printer separately, then you have to install a driver. This, incidentally, is one of the advantages of using Windows. In the days BW (Before Windows), you would have to install a printer driver for each program that might use the printer. Using Windows, you install one driver for Windows, and all the programs that use Windows also use this driver.

- If you use any programs that require MS-DOS directly, they cannot use the Windows driver. If they need to use the printer you will have to use the driver that belongs to the program. Fortunately, you are not likely to have any programs of that type unless you collect antique computers.

To install a Windows driver for your printer:

1   Click the *Start* button, or press the Flag key if you have one.

2   Move the pointer to *Settings*, and click on *Control Panel*.

3   When the Control Panel appears, **double-click** on *Printers*.

4   In the new panel that appears, **double-click** on *Add Printer*.

5   You will see the *Add Printer Wizard* appear, with instructions. Follow the instructions to see a list of manufacturers and models. Select the manufacturer of your printer (such as Epson, Canon, Hewlett-Packard, Lexmark, etc.) and then the model. If in doubt, look at the box the printer came in.

6   The driver for that printer will be installed, and you can click the box that is marked *Default printer*. This ensures that even if you install another driver, the first one will always be used unless you specify otherwise.

Once the driver has been installed, your printer can be used with any of your Windows software. All software that permits printing will have its own ways of carrying out the printing of a document. The two most common methods are:

• Clicking an icon of a printer that appears in a toolbar, often at the top of the screen.

• Using a *File* menu that contains a *Print* item, and clicking on *Print*.

Printers

Many programs use both methods. Usually, clicking the printer icon will print all of the document that the program is working on. Using the File — Print menu steps allow you to choose what you want to print for a list such as *All*, *This page*, *Selected text*, *Even pages*, *Odd pages*, and so on.

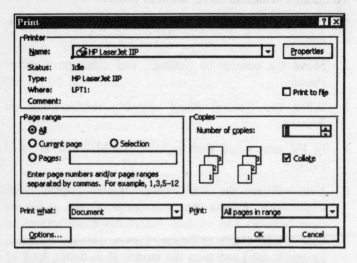

- The printer must be loaded with paper and switched on (*online*) when you use the Print command or click the printer icon. Using Windows 95, you will see a screen message appear if the printer is not online or is out of paper, and the printer will start working when you have attended to it.

- If you are using drawing or painting programs, the printing routines are usually more elaborate, allowing you to alter the scale of the drawing to fit a full page or part of a page.

Care of the printer

Printers are not temperamental devices, and they need only a small amount of care. The main item of care is to ensure that dust does not gather, and for some type of printers a dust-cover is a useful investment. On other models, all openings are either underneath or well covered so that dust has very little effect on them, and no cover is needed.

Inkjet and laser printers need very little care apart from replenishing supplies. Be guided by the manufacturer, who may specify that you dust lightly inside the printer each time you change the ink or toner. Never use any liquid cleaners or polishes, particularly sprays, because these can damage printer parts. Keep rollers clean — the liquid used for cleaning spectacle lenses is usually suitable, but be guided by the instructions that come with the printer.

Sometimes a laser printer will produce sheets that are stained on one side. This is usually a sign that the toner has spilled on to a roller, and the remedy depends on the way that the printer is designed. The Hewlett-Packard Laserjet designs, for example, are very easy to service because most of the parts that need replacement are inside a cartridge that also carries the toner, so that each time you replenish the toner you are renewing almost everything that can give trouble. Rollers can be cleaned by unclipping them and washing in soapy water, then allowing to dry naturally.

Several inkjet machines use a combined ink reservoir and jet block, so that renewing this deals with any problems of clogged jets. Other machines allow the ink to be replenished leaving the jets in place, and you need replace the jets only if you see evidence that one or more jets is clogged (missing bits of printed characters, for example).

The older dot-matrix printers may need more cleaning, because the printing head is more exposed, and can become clogged with fibre from the ribbon. To some extent, replacing an old ribbon will clean the head, but you may need to brush the head clean at intervals. Once again, the manufacturer's instructions must be followed, and the problem is that you might not have a copy of these instructions. A plea for help to one of the computing magazines will often produce a sheaf of letters offering to send a manual for your older model of printer.

Replenishing supplies

Supplies for a printer, other than paper, mean ink for inkjets, toner for laser printers, and ribbons for dot-matrix types. You normally have the choice of buying makers' original supplies, supplies from other manufacturers, or recycled supplies. I might be unlucky, but I have never been able to get more than a few pages of print from recycled laser cartridges, and some would not even print that much. I save money now by avoiding them.

Both toner and ink are far from cheap. Toner for laser printers is a very fine powder, often a mixture of the marking material with magnetic material, and you should not be tempted to try to recharge a laser printer with toner. The fine powder is a hazard to your lungs and is difficult to clean up if you spill it — it will pass through any vacuum-cleaner bag unless you use a cleaner of the Medivac or Nilfisk class. Another point is that though you can wash it away using cold water and soap, hot water will melt it into place and you will never remove the stain.

Ink for inkjet printers is not the ink that you can buy for fountain pens (remember them?), but a specially formulated form of ink that dries as soon as it hits the paper. It has also to be free from small particles, because the jets in the printing head are finer than a human hair and are easily clogged. Ink of this type is not cheap, and you do not get many sheets of paper from a filling — in this respect, different makes and models vary greatly, and some have much larger ink reservoirs than others.

The computing magazines are full of offers of replacement ink cartridges and refilling systems, and whether you take these up or not depends on how much printing you intend to do, and how good you are at working with small parts. Some refilling systems use hypodermic needles, and you might not want to have such things in your house.

Dot-matrix printers need attention when the print becomes faint, and the easiest remedy is to fit a new ribbon. Some types use a long ribbon in a wide cartridge, and such ribbons usually have a long life. Others, particularly some 24-pin printers, have short ribbons with an equally short life. You can re-ink ribbons for yourself, but this is worth while only for the longer ribbons, because the short ribbons usually wear badly and jam the printer if you try to re-use them.

Paper for your printer

Printers should not need special paper unless your printing requirements are unusual. If you are concerned with printing pictures of photographic quality on a colour ink-jet or one of the specialised wax or dye printers, then you will need very costly paper, which can cost as much as 10p per sheet.

Most of us, however, get by with photocopy paper at £2.50 or less per ream (500 sheets) of A4 size. This is ideal for laser printers (because a photocopier is a type of laser printer) and should be suitable for all but the more fussy inkjets. Avoid any printer that needs special paper, because the paper price may rise steadily and there is nothing you can do about it. This is particularly important if, like me, you reckon to get through 30 or more reams in a year.

Never buy a vast amount of paper (to get the best discount rates) until you have put a few sheets through your printer. I keep a file of a finely-detailed drawing that I use to test paper — if it comes out looking crisp and clear I'll buy the paper, if it looks fuzzy I'll try another batch.

7 Using your software

All the software that you are likely to use will run using Windows, and nowadays this means Windows 95 or 98 except for older machines. One great advantage of using Windows is that you do not need to learn many new tricks for new programs — the familiar clicking and dragging actions are used in all programs that run under Windows.

Some of your software will already have been installed, and we have looked already at how new software is added. As you become more familiar with your software you might want to upgrade to a new version, to change to a different program that carries out the same task, or to try software that does something new and unfamiliar to you.

Whatever you choose, you will recognise features that are common to all Windows software. These include menus, toolbars, scroll bars and a status bar.

A **menu** is a list of commands or options, and the conventional method is to have a line of main menu titles at the top of the screen. For example, Microsoft Word 97 uses the list *File*, *Edit*, *View*, *Insert*, *Format*, *Tools*, *Table*, *Window* and *Help*. Practically all programs will have *File*, *Windows* and *Help* menus, but other names will be different if the program has a different purpose.

The use of **toolbars** is usually a (faster) alternative to using menus rather than a replacement. A toolbar consists of a set of icons, and you carry out an action by clicking an icon rather than a word in a menu. Some programs make a lot of use of toolbars, and allow you to conceal them or reveal them as you choose. For example Word 97 can use 14 or more toolbars, but you normally work with just two. The PagePlus DTP program is another that can use a large number of toolbars. Some programs will make a toolbar appear automatically when you start an action, such as drawing a picture into a word-processed document, that can make good use of a toolbar.

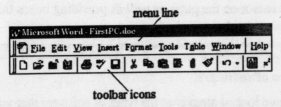

menu line

toolbar icons

Scroll bars are used to overcome the fact that the screen size is usually not the same as the size of paper you will print on. A scroll bar has a square 'slider' that can be dragged up and down, using the mouse. When you drag this slider up, its like dragging paper down — you move towards the start of the document. Dragging the slider down moves you towards the end of the document. There are arrowheads at each end of the bar that can be clicked to provide small movements of a set size in each direction.

slider

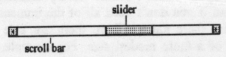

scroll bar

Some programs provide both a vertical and a horizontal scroll bar, so that you can see all of a wide document by dragging the slider on the horizontal bar. This is particularly useful for drawing programs that can create a drawing that is much larger than the screen. This allows you to work on a magnified version of a drawing, seeing detail that is invisible in a normal screen view. The horizontal type has been illustrated above.

The **status bar** is placed at the bottom of the screen, and it contain information. For a word processor, for example, the status bar would typically show the current page number, section number, total number of pages, position of the pointer (line and column) and might also contain some icons that could be clicked to produce special actions. The example illustrated is from Microsoft Word, and it shows items such as page number, section number and the position of the cursor on the page, as well as providing boxes that can be clicked to change actions.

Types of software

We have looked already at the types of software that you can use, and in this section we'll look in more detail, now that you have more experience of the computer and of Windows.

Word processing is one of the main uses of computers, and there are three big-name word-processing programs. These are Microsoft Word, Corel WordPerfect, and Lotus Word Pro. It's likely that you will have had one of these bundled with your new computer, or that there is a word-processing portion to an all-in-one program such as Microsoft Works.

These are by no means the only word processing programs around, and if you don't need all of the immense range of actions that these can perform, there are able (and fast) programs of a more modest size. For example, WordPad, which is part of Windows 95, provides all that you might need at this stage, and creates files that are compatible with Word 97 if you later upgrade. Let's look at the features that you might expect from word processors.

All will, of course, allow you to type words and edit your work, deleting, moving and altering text. You can save your text to a folder in the hard drive or to a floppy, and read the text in again when you want to alter it or use it for another purpose. All will allow you to choose fonts (the type of lettering), and to position your text neatly on the page, using tabulation stops as required. All will allow you to emphasise words or phrases, using **bold** type or *italics* as required, perhaps also <u>underlining</u>. The actions will be visible on the screen; you do not have to wait until you print the text before seeing how it looks. This illustrates the feature called WYSIWYG, meaning what you see is what you get. There is no need to print on paper until you are certain that the document is perfect.

One feature that used to be provided on only the top-end programs is now common on all except the budget varieties. Spell-checking allows you to check each word in a document and either alter it by hand or use a suggested replacement if it looks incorrectly spelled. The spell-checker will allow you to add new words, such as proper names or specialised terms, so that they are not questioned again. The first spell-checkers were not very good, but the modern versions are excellent, and even if your spelling is superb (meaning that you are aged 60 or over) they catch mis-typing as well as mis-spelling, though none of the smaller ones can find a word that is used incorrectly, such as *inn* in place of *in*. By contrast, Word allows you to keep a list of such words and query them as if they were incorrectly spelled.

Even the simple and low-cost word processing software will provide a range of useful actions, so what do you get in the larger varieties? One important addition is the ability to create tables. The smaller programs can create tables only by using tabulation stops (tabs), and you can spend a lot of time adjusting stop positions before you obtain a neat looking tables. On the larger programs this is all automatic, and creating tables become so easy that you seldom use tabs at all.

All three top-line programs can perform the tasks listed below, and the lower-cost programs can perform some of these tasks, so you can get some idea of what to look for. Very few users need even 50% of the facilities of the big three, but almost everybody needs a different set of these requirements, which is why the big three are so popular in offices where each user has different needs.

Using your software

Templates are files that hold details of a document. By using a template you can create an instant document, ready to add detail. You can create templates for fax sheets, letters, memos, invoices, etc., so that each document that you create can conform to the pattern that you want to use.

Grammar-checking is a relatively new feature of word processors, and one that still needs work done. The English language cannot be summed up in a few simple rules, so that grammar checker software will often show as faulty a sentence that is perfectly acceptable, and also fail to find one that is grossly ungrammatical. At the present stage of development, the grammar checker is useful to find omitted full stops or other punctuation faults, but it should not be relied on to correct your grammar for you.

Thesaurus action will provide alternatives to a word that you select. You can use this to provide variety in your text by avoiding repetition of a word, or to provide a different emphasis such as by using, for example, *task* in place of *work*, a word with a more weighty meaning. All Thesaurus programs will provide a meaning and a list of *synonyms*, words with the same or similar meaning, and some will also provide *antonyms*, words with an opposite meaning.

Columns, meaning newspaper columns rather than table columns, can be specified. When you opt for newspaper columns, the story starts at the top of the left-hand column of a page and continues down that column. At the end of the left-hand column, the story continues in the next column to the right, and so on. The use of newspaper columns was at one time possible only if you used DTP software, but it is now a common feature of top-end word processors.

Merge actions of various types are also possible. You can add the text of one document to another, or you can compare two similar documents and pick portions of each to put into a final document. You can also merge in different types of documents, such as tables from a spreadsheet.

Graphics abilities are a very important part of the action of any high-level word processing software. You can place a picture file of any recognised type into your text document so that the text will be printed with the illustrations that you include. These graphics can be embedded or linked. An *embedded* graphics file is added to the document, so that the document takes up more space in the memory and in the hard drive. When a graphics file is *linked*, only a small amount of additional memory is needed in the document, because the original graphics file is used to provide the information when the document is viewed or printed. This makes the document file much shorter than one which contains the same files embedded, but you have to be careful not to move or rename the graphics files.

Accounts

Keeping accounts can be very tedious when you use paper, mainly because making corrections is so difficult. Since bookkeeping software was introduced, it has rapidly become popular for small-business and personal use, so that accounts programs are now near the top of the list of most-used software. You should distinguish between bookkeeping and accounts. Bookkeeping means entering and storing each financial transaction, whether by cash, cheque, credit or debit card, or electronic transfer. You can create as many accounts as you need, show the transactions in each, transfer between accounts, show balances, etc. As you might expect, the information can be displayed on screen and also printed.

The accountancy portion of these programs deals with more than just the entry of transactions. It is concerned, for example, with growth of investments, budgeting, reporting and other aspects of money management. No accounts program, however, can truly replace the work of an accountant in advising on investment, taxation, pension funds and other matters that require judgement as well as rules.

Using your software

Games

Games exist in a large number of varieties, some calling for manual skills, others for thought. At one time it was thought that no small computer could ever match a human chess-player, but there are now many programs that will give even a good player a pretty hard time, and many will also cater for the beginner by playing the game on a simpler level. Many other board games, such as Bridge and Mahjongg can be obtained in computer form, and they all have the advantage that a game which is interrupted can be stored so that you can resume it later. Word games, quizzes, and card games are also popular.

Adventure games, unlike the board games, scarcely existed before computers. An adventure game outlines a situation in which the player is placed, usually with the help of illustrations. You might, for example, be in a forest clearing, a cave, a runaway train, even a moon of Mars. You have to get to some destination by typing commands or choosing options, and you can gain points by making good decisions. On your way, you can pick up items that are offered (axes, spears, books, maps, etc.) and which may be useful later. Maximum points are awarded for getting to the destination quickly, and on most adventure games this is by no means easy, calling for abilities similar to those needed for crosswords. There may be thousands of situations (or 'rooms') that can be encountered in the course of one adventure, so that no two games ever develop in an identical way.

Arcade games are the type that gave computers a bad name at one time, and which are generally noisy, pointless and addictive. The typical arcade game shows some form of attack, usually by aliens, and invites you to shoot down the invaders. A joystick is a considerable advantage, because these games are clumsy if you can use only the keyboard or mouse to control the actions.

The better type of arcade games call for some thought as well as fast reactions, and manufacturers have not been slow to adapt the principles of arcade games to educational programs that can be useful in training.

Simulation games are a development of arcade games, in which the screen shows a simulation of items such as an aircraft flight deck, a railway signal box, the bridge of a warship, the control room of a power station, or other similar control centres. You are in control, and various events unfold that call for you to operate the controls to ensure survival. Some of the flight simulation software can be uncannily good, and only the feeling of being airborne is absent.

Strategy games encompass such actions as finding your way through a maze, arranging blocks into a pattern, and forms of board games that exist only in computer form. There are also programs for creating your own games, and programs for war-gaming.

Multimedia

Multimedia software needs a computer that is equipped with a fast CD-ROM drive, along with a sound card and loudspeakers. Virtually all modern computers come with a CD-ROM drive, and only machines that are sold for purely business purposes omit the sound card and loudspeaker (which can easily be added later).

The best-known type of multimedia software is the encyclopædia, and this is also the type of software that is most often bundled along with a new computer. The quality of encyclopædia software varies considerably, and you cannot assume that because the paper version of an encyclopædia is good that the computer version will also be good. Another point to note is that many multimedia encyclopædias are heavily biased to US users, so that anything European is likely to be either ignored or glossed unless it is essential. The Hutchinson encyclopædia is of UK origin, and the later versions of Microsoft Encarta are adapted for UK tastes.

In addition, the displays and methods of different encyclopædias vary considerably. In this respect, Microsoft Encarta is so far unbeaten in being easy and interesting to use, with an excellent range of pictures and sounds. This does not mean that all topics are explained in a simple way, and you may find in many encyclopædias that children may not be able to make much of some of the topics. If you want multimedia software for the exclusive use of children, look first at some of the titles from Dorling Kindersley.

Multimedia educational programs account for a large number of the titles that are issued, and the better examples are of considerable use in both teaching new material and in reinforcing items that have been previously learned. The advantage of multimedia methods is that testing and revising can be made more interesting and that the user can work with the computer without the need for supervision or prompting. The advantages of multimedia are best utilised, to date, in topics that broadly come under the 'science' heading, such as Chemistry, Physics and Biology, Geography, Environmental studies, and Mathematics.

Animated stories for children are a rapidly-growing application for multimedia, though to date most tend to be US-biased. These compete for children's attention with cartoons on video, and the advantage of the multimedia version is that some degree of interaction is possible, allowing the user to vary the unwrapping of the story (it's better than just shouting 'look behind you').

Reference works are often well-adapted to multimedia format, and the encyclopædia is just one outstanding example. Art and Nature are particularly popular topics for this form of software, but more mundane items like route-finders and hotel guides can be placed under this heading.

Gardening is a particularly popular topic for multimedia in the UK.

Music is a fast-growing area of interest for multimedia. The obvious areas of lives and works of the great composers are well covered, but you can also obtain information on musical instruments, tuition in music theory, and even guidance on composition from multimedia discs.

Special interest is a heading that covers a variety of topics, ranging from amateur radio to needlecraft, that are of interest to a large number of users, but not to such large numbers as are attracted to the more general works.

Note that lists often show sources rather than topics, and it is not always easy to find exactly what you want. In addition, when lists are arranged under topic headings, some titles may appear in several different sections. Some Internet sites can display selected portion of multimedia works so that you can browse without buying. This can be useful if you don't want to buy a complete encyclopædia just to look up one item, and you can also use the facility to decide whether a title on CD would be useful to you.

If you buy multimedia titles in North America the prices will be much lower, but you should insist on seeing the CD working on a computer system similar to your own. Some of the lower-priced discs, for example, will run only with Windows 3.1, and cannot be easily adapted for Windows 95 or 98.

Using multimedia programs

To use a multimedia program, you must first have installed the software. The CD-ROM that contains the program is inserted into its drive, and you run an installation or setup program. This places some files on your hard drive, and makes the use of the multimedia files much easier and faster than it would be if you had to run everything from the CD-ROM drive.

Using your software

Once the multimedia program has been installed, you can use it with the CD in the drive. The files are read from the CD into the memory of your computer as needed, and for some types of program, particularly those that use animated pictures and sound, you need a fast CD-ROM drive. Jerky animation usually means that either the CD-ROM drive is too slow, or that you need a faster graphics card on your computer.

Copying text, sound, and pictures is usually possible, subject to copyright restrictions. Most multimedia pages contain a *Print* button that can be clicked to print out the current page, and it is equally common to have a *Copy* button that can be clicked to copy the text and/or pictures. If you then switch to a word processor, you can use the *Paste* button or command to make a copy of the multimedia page as a word-processor document.

If you want to copy the sound from a multimedia you will need to connect a cassette recorder to the *Line out* socket of the sound card in your computer. With the recorder switched to *Record*, play the multimedia sound, and then press the *Stop* key on the recorder when the sound ends. Rewind the tape and replay it to hear what you have recorded. Remember that the sound content of multimedia discs is also subject to copyright.

- In general, copying is permitted if it is purely for your own private uses, but you must not attempt to broadcast, display, sell or hire out such material.

Internet

The Internet has for some time been the buzzword in computing, and computers nowadays come with all the necessary equipment for connecting to the Internet. The hardware consists of a *modem*, a gadget that converts outgoing computer signals into tones that can be transmitted along telephone lines and incoming tones into computer signals, allowing two-way communication. The software consists of a set of programs that control the main Internet actions of browsing, Email and news. The most frequently supplied software is either Microsoft Internet Explorer or Netscape Navigator.

In addition to the hardware and software, you need to sign up with an information provider (IP), someone whose (large) computer you connect to when you want to use the Internet. There are many IPs available at a range of prices, and because the whole process is very competitive (and potentially very profitable) there are many free offers. You can get away with using the Internet for a year or so if you simply move from one free offer to another, but most users soon find an IP that provides what they want at a reasonable price. If your main need is Email, you should find an IP that offers very low cost services (£5 per month or less) rather than one which offers unlimited time for sums of three times this amount. Remember that you need an IP which you can contact at local telephone rates, because all the time you use the Internet (the buzzword is *online*) you are using your telephone line.

- If you use Email, changing your IP requires you to change your Email filename (address), so that you have to inform everyone who might want to contact you.

Browsing means looking for information or entertainment. Because there is such a vast range of data on the Internet you need some assistance in finding anything you want, so that a key part of your software consists of some way of searching and selecting the portions that you want. Even so, a simple query might result in several thousand references, and the more specific you can be the better. The software that carries out the searching is called a 'search engine' and is not part of your own software — it will be located on some large computer that is also connected to the Internet, so that your

83

own software simply converts your request into signals that the search engine can deal with. These search engines are named, using titles like Alta Vista, Lycos, Infoseek and so on.

Some IPs, notably the large US-based IPs such as MSN, and AOL, along with BT in the UK, provide software that contains additional services such as entertainment, financial news, world news, shopping services, etc. If you want these services from the Internet, you might find that signing up with these IPs provides a less costly way of obtaining these services. On the other hand, if you do not want the services it is pointless to pay for them, though some IPs will allow you a low-access contract, paying around £5 per month for a limited number of hours online, with excess time charged by the hour. This can be useful if your main need is for Email, with only a limited amount of browsing from time to time.

Internet documents look like the more familiar form of computer documents, but they contain *hyperlinks*. These hyperlinks are icons or pieces of coloured text that you can click on. When you click on a hyperlink, you connect to another document. For example, if you are reading a document about Egypt, clicking on the word **pyramid** that appears in colour will switch you to anther document about pyramids. The use of hyperlinks allows you to chase information from one document to another, and the software allows you to go back over the documents you have viewed (whether you are online or not). It is this use of hyperlinks that allows the popular action of *surfing*, chasing information from one reference to another.

Email is the most common reason for starting an Internet connection. When you send Email, you use a word-processor (or text editor, which might be part of your Internet software) to generate your letter, and then use a *Send* command while you are connected to the Internet. This sends the document, in coded form, to be stored at the computer used by your IP, and the sending time is very brief, only a few seconds. You can terminate the Internet connection as soon as you have dealt with the Email, saving on connection time, because if there is any incoming Email for you it will also be read while you are online. The Email that you have sent out will reach its destination when your contact goes online.

One huge advantage of Email, as compared, for example, to fax, is that you do not need to keep your computer switched on and connected, because an incoming Email will reach you whenever you go online. In addition, Email is much faster, and you don't need to print it unless you want to. The cost of Email is also much lower if you use the service to a reasonable extent.

News services on the Internet are really chat services, and they are organised into groups on the basis of some special interest. The idea is that each member of a group can contribute, and this can often be a fruitful way of resolving a problem. It can also be a way of starting an argument that can become abusive, pointless and never-ending, so that the News facility is one that needs to be used with care and with some regard to established rules of polite behaviour (no matter how you see others behave).

The Internet is what you make of it. Searching for the answer to a problem can be exhilarating or tedious, and you have to resign yourself to learning how to use what is available — for example, which search engine performs best on the type of questions you pose it. The main danger is that you can waste a great deal of time and hard-earned cash on endlessly chasing items that interest you without finding anything that is of real use.

Appendix A

Glossary of abbreviations

This is a small list of commonly-used abbreviations that applies particularly to terms currently used in Windows and MS-DOS 6.0. For a full explanation of terms used in computing, see Collins *Dictionary of Personal Computing* by Ian Sinclair.

ANSI American National Standards Institute. The title is used for a number code system that follows the ASCII set for numbers 32 to 127, and which also specifies characters for the set 128 to 255.

ASCII American Standard Code for Information Interchange, the number code for letters, numerals and punctuation marks that uses the numbers 32 to 127. Text files are normally ASCII or ANSI coded.

AT Advanced Technology, the designation used by IBM in 1982 for the computer that followed the PC-XT. See also ISA.

BIOS Basic Input Output System, the program in a ROM chip that allows the computer to make use of screen, disc and keyboard, and which can read in the operating system.

CAD Computer Aided Design, a program that allows the computer to produce technical drawings to scale.

CD-ROM A form of read-only memory, consisting of a compact disc whose digital information can be read as a set of files.

CGA Colour Graphics Adapter, the first IBM attempt to produce a video graphics card, now out of date.

CISC Complex Instruction Set Chip, a microprocessor which can act on any of a very large number (typically more than 300) instructions. All of the Intel microprocessors to date are of this type. See also RISC.

CMOS Complementary Metal-Oxide Semiconductor, a form of chip construction that requires a very low current. As applied to memory, a chip that allows its contents to be retained by applying a low voltage at negligible current.

COM 1 Abbreviation for Communication used to indicate a serial port. The COM ports are numbered as COM1, COM2 etc. 2 An extension for a short type of program file.

CP/M Control, Program, Monitor, one of the first standard operating systems for small computers.

CPU Central Processing Unit, the main microprocessor chip of a computer.

CRT Cathode Ray Tube, the display device for monitors used with desktop machines.

CTS Clear To Send, the companion handshake signal to RTS in the RS-232 system.

DCE Data Communications Equipment, a device such as a computer that send out serial data along a line.

DIL Dual In Line, a pin arrangement for chips that uses two sets of parallel pins.

DIMM A package used for memory chips using 168 pins. See also SIMM.

DIP Dual in Line Package, a set of miniature switches arranged in the same form of package as a DIL chip.

DOS Disc Operating System, the programs that provides the commands that make a computer usable.

DSR Data Set Ready, another form of handshaking signals for RS-232.

Glossary

DTE   Data Terminal Equipment, a receiver of serial data such as a modem.

DTR   Data Terminal Ready, the RS232 companion signals to DSR.

DTP   Desktop Publishing, the use of a computer for composing type and graphics into book or newspaper pages.

EGA   Enhanced Graphics Adapter, the improved form of graphics card introduced by IBM to replace the old CGA system.

EISA   Enhanced Industry Standard Architecture, a system for connecting chips in a PC machine which allows faster signal interchange than the standard (ISA) method that has been used since the early PC/AT models.

IDSN   A fast-acting form of connection used by businesses to communicate digital data. The letters mean integrated services digital network, and ISDN lines are supplied by BT.

ISA   Industry Standard Architecture, meaning the design methods used in the IBM PC/AT model, which have become a standard. A modified version of this is called EISA, meaning extended ISA.

LCD   Liquid Crystal Display, a form of shadow display which is used on calculators and portable computers. It depends on the action of materials to polarise light when an electrical voltage is applied.

LCS   Liquid Crystal Shutter, an array of LCD elements used to control light and so expose the light-sensitive drum in a laser printer. The LCD bar is used as an alternative to the use of a laser beam.

LED   Light Emitting Diode, a device used for warning lights, and also as a form of light source in laser-style printers.

LPT An abbreviation of *Line Printer*, used to mean the parallel port (also indicated by PRN). When more than one parallel port is available, these will be numbered as LPT1, LPT2, etc.

MIDI Musical Instrument Digital Interface, a standard form of serial data code used to allow electronic instruments to be controlled by a computer, or to link them with each other.

MSD The Microsoft System diagnosis utility of Windows 3.1 which will prepare a report on your system on screen, on paper or as a text file.

MS-DOS Microsoft Disc Operating System, the standard operating system for the PC type of machine.

NTSC National Television Standards Committee, the body that drew up the specification for the colour TV system used in the USA and Japan since 1952. NTSC TV signals cannot be used on PAL (UK) receivers, which is why you cannot play videotapes you bought in the USA unless you have a video player and TV that can be used with NTSC tapes.

OCR Optical Character Recognition, software that can be used on a scanned image file to convert images of characters into ASCII codes.

OS/2 An operating system devised by IBM and intended to replace PC-DOS (the IBM version of MS-DOS).

PAL Phase Alternating Line, the colour TV system devised by Telefunken in Germany and used throughout Europe apart from France.

PBX Private Branch Exchange, sometimes a problem for using modems.

PSS Packet Switch Stream, a method of transmitting digital signals efficiently along telephone lines.

Glossary

RAM Random Access Memory. All memory is random-access, but this acronym is used to mean read-write as distinct from read-only memory.

RGB Red Green Blue, the three primary colour TV signals. A monitor described as RGB needs to be supplied with three separate colour signals, unlike a monitor that can use a composite signal.

RISC a microprocessor that can work with only a few simple instructions, each of which can be completed very rapidly.

RLL Run Length Limited, a form of high-density recording for hard discs.

ROM Read-Only Memory, the form of non-volatile memory that is not erased when the power is switched off.

RS232 The old-established standard for serial (one bit at a time) communications. Computers use a modified form of RS-232 from connection to modems.

RTS Request to Send, a handshaking signal for RS-232.

SCART The standard form of connector for video equipment, used on TV receivers and video recorders.

SCSI Small Computer Systems Interface, a form of fast-acting disc drive interface which allows for almost unlimited expansion.

SECAM Sequence Colour et Memoire, the French colour TV system, also used in Eastern Europe and the countries of the former USSR. Secam TV signals cannot be viewed on a PAL receiver (as used in the UK).

SIMM Single Inline Memory Module, a slim card carrying memory chips, used for inserting memory in units of 1, 4, 8, 16 and 32 Mbyte.

TIFF   Tagged Image File Format, one method of coding graphics images that is widely used by scanners.

TSR   Terminate and Stray Resident, a form of program that runs and remains in the memory to influence the computer.

TTL   Transistor-Transistor Logic, a family of digital chips. The name is often used to mean that a device will work on 0 and +5V levels.

VDU   Visual Display Unit, another name for the monitor.

VEGA Video Extended Graphics Association, a group of US manufacturers who have agreed on a common standard for high-resolution graphics cards

VGA   Video Graphics Array, the video card originally introduced by IBM for their PS/2 range of computers, and now a standard. An extended version is called SVGA, with the letter S meaning Super.

Index

Index

Index

Notes

Notes